HERE, THERE, &
OTHERWHERE . . .
AN ORDINARY WOMAN AT EXTRAORDINARY TIMES

VOLUME TWO

Other books by Phyl Manning:

Arctic Circles
Kalana Press, 2013

Here, There and Otherwhere, Volume 1
Kalana Press, 2013

Here is the African Jungle
Illustrated by Steve Ferchaud
Wizard Graphics, 2006

Kiti: A Historical Tale of the Traditional Inupiat
Kalana Press, 2013

HERE, THERE, & OTHERWHERE...

AN ORDINARY WOMAN AT EXTRAORDINARY TIMES

VOLUME TWO

PHYL MANNING

(signature)

Phyl's bOOks

Wilton, New Hampshire

Here, There & Otherwhere . . .

AN ORDINARY WOMAN AT EXTRAORDINARY TIMES

Volume 2

by

Phyl Manning

Paperback ISBN 13: 978-1-62742-000-6
Mobi (Kindle) ISBN 13: 978-1-62742-001-3
ePub (Sony, Nook, iPad) ISBN 13: 978-1-62742-002-0

Author's Note: This is a work of narrative nonfiction. These stories are drawn from memories of events that have happened during the course of my life. In telling these stories, I have tried to be truthful and to paint an accurate picture of events as they occurred. Memory, however, is an imperfect thing and any additions or omissions are my own.

Cover Design by Irene Farrar, 23 Tons, inc.
Front Cover Sculpture by Carolyn C. Boutwell
Author Photo by Douglas P. Bratten
Tiger Photograph by Sultana Saritaş
Interior Design by Pam Marin-Kingsley

Animal Backgrounds (5) and Tiger Photo Subject Supplied through
Kirshner Wildlife & Educational Center
4995 Durham-Pentz Road
Oroville, CA 95965
Phone: (530) 553-1000

Phyl's bOOks

an imprint of
Kalana Press
PO Box 377
Wilton, NH 03086
www.phylsbooks.com
www.kalanapress.com

In Loving Memory of
William Keith Moore
. . . the Dear Cousin
Who Shared
My Earliest
Adventures

Contents

1

. . . .

(Beattie, Kansas)

Sex Education

The sun is brilliant, the temperature is hot even for July, and I am peeking down at the driveway through the window of our attic bedroom. Waves of shimmering air rise up from my Mother's Chevy named Genevieve and also from my aunt and uncle's nameless old Ford. A lake of gray-brown dust lies where the front yard was green last summer. Mother and I got here from Omaha three days ago to spend the rest of this summer on the Kansas farm.

Mother is up here with me for an after-lunch rest. And Mother has a Mission.

"Children who grow up on farms are much more knowledgeable about life and how it continues." My mother sits in a platform rocker near the window. She is fanning herself with a yellowed issue of *Capper's Weekly*. I can spot the numbers "1936" on the dateline, but am still unable to read the month printed there.

"Those who grow up in the city," she continues, "have no inkling about—well, about reproduction."

Mother is a school teacher and always expects me to answer. But she hasn't asked a question. I am content to turn attention to a spider web spun in an orange crate on end under the window.

"I've decided that it's time for you to have your questions answered," Mother announces.

But I notice that a fly is caught in the web. I watch it struggle, put my hand in slowly to help, but then withdraw it draped with a bit of the sticky stuff clinging because that simple bit of motion agitates the insect even more.

"So you just ask questions, Honey, and I'll try to answer them."

I do notice that a black and yellow spider, quite large, is clinging to the edge of the web.

"Go ahead, Dear. Ask me anything."

"Why is a garden spider in the attic?"

"No, I mean questions about reproduction."

"What's reproduction?"

"Bearing young. You know how Krissy has puppies? That's to make sure there'll be more dogs after she grows old and is finally gone."

"I've seen black and yellow spiders like this in the garden at home. Here, too, in weeds by the outhouse and over by the silo."

"Don't you ever wonder, though?"

"About what?"

"Reproduction."

"No."

"But you're almost five! Of course you want to know how babies are made."

I am warned by growing exasperation in my parent's voice. I wonder what I'm supposed to be saying or doing. Something. That I know. "By having married people love each other, if they aren't too old?"

"Yes, well, and that's all you think you need to know?"

Mother wants more from me, and I realize that. But honestly, I've just now decided definitely that I like spiders better than flies.

Now I watch the garden spider move slowly out onto the web.

Mother laughs. "Here I get myself all steeled to talk to you about love and babies—"

"—How old do I have to be to get married and have babies?" I ask hopefully.

"Lots older than five, Sweetheart. Maybe twenty-three or twenty-five or even thirty. After you're through college."

That's pretty much what I thought—not soon.

"You shouldn't wait the way I did, though," Mother continues. "Thirty-five with my first child, and the doctor said I'd never have another."

Mother's voice is suddenly warm and happy. "But I had you, and you're all I need. Your papa was nearly fifty when you were born."

"How old do spiders get to be?" I wonder aloud.

"He'd had some children before, naturally. But his first wife wasn't too well. She had three but died with the third one. So she passed on."

"Do spiders have babies or lay eggs?" I ask.

"Listen, when I was young, the word 'baby' was hardly mentioned in our house. Except that my mother kept having them. I was the eldest girl of the three who lived. Five total with the boys."

"Uh-hmm." I hope that spiders have babies the way Krissy does. If they lay eggs like chickens, then the little ones are sure to be lonely.

"Legs were *limbs*, in those days. And bosoms were *chest*—same word for everyone, man and woman, though of course they're not at all the same. I don't want to be like that with you, my dear."

Still, fuzzy little chicks swarm all around their mama hen after they hatch. Maybe laying eggs isn't so bad, after all.

"Phyllis?"

"Yes, Mother." When she uses my full name, I know she wants my attention. But the spider is moving closer to the fly, and the fly has stopped struggling.

"My own mother led me to believe that having sex is a terrible thing, that it's painful and dirty and disgusting."

"What's sex?"

"Reproduction."

"Oh." How can the spider move in so silently, without seeming to move at all? Like tiptoeing—only spiders don't have toes, do they?

"And you can imagine my amazement, when I finally married just to have a child and in spite of my dread, only to discover that sex—uh, reproduction, isn't like that at all."

The two front legs are moving the spider ever so slowly forward toward the fly.

"Not that I didn't love your papa, you understand. And I love him even more now. But we could have just been good friends, as we already were, seeing each other and talking at church on Sunday and after prayer meeting on Wednesday evening . . . except that I wanted, really *wanted* to have a baby."

I startle back when the spider pounces. I guess the larger insect will eat the smaller one. Or maybe the fly will be stored away like squirrels hide nuts and acorns.

"And Adolph was lonely after his first wife was gone—see? I do it still! And with death. . . . We say that people who die 'pass away' or 'depart' or 'are taken,' or 'are gone.' That's silly. They *die*, stop breathing and go to heaven or hell. In our family—which was a good, decent one, hard-working and sober farmer folk all—we used a lot of peculiar words to avoid subjects considered taboo."

"Taboo, taboo, taboo." I really do like the sound of the word and the feel of it on my tongue. "What's a taboo, taboo, taboo?"

"Not to be talked about. And one taboo was sex."

"What's sex—oh, reproduction. Like Krissy." Nothing much seems to be happening with the spider now that it has drawn the fly to it.

"If you had an inkling of how hard it is for me to talk about these matters, Phyl—"

"—What matters?"

"—And how rarely I'm going to be able to do so, then you'd bombard me with questions."

"What's bombard?"

"Hitting over and again—as with guns or snowballs or questions. You'd be asking me lots and lots of questions."

"About what?" I can still see a part of the fly, but most of it seems to be under the spider. I notice suddenly that there is silence in the room.

Then Mother says, "Reproduction."

"Oh."

"Is it possible that you're too young?"

"I'm not too young for lots of things!" My defense is automatic. "I can ride horseback." And now only the tiniest part of the fly is visible.

Mother hoists herself from the rocker, walks over. "Just remember, Honey, that when you're married, anything your husband and you want to do together is all right. It's a wonderful experience, making a baby or not. . . . Do you understand any part of what I'm talking about?"

Mother lowers herself awkwardly onto the floor, her arms helping her large flesh get down to sit beside me.

"What has been the subject of our conversation?" she asks me.

"Reproduction," I answer promptly.

Mother reaches her left arm out, draws me over for a big hug. "File it away," she tells me, then laughs, "and bring it out when you need it."

Then Mother releases me and hunkers herself forward to peer closely at the web. "What do we have here?"

"A spider, and it just caught a fly."

"Will you look at that!" Mother says in some awe. "What in the world is a garden spider doing 'way up here in the attic?"

2

The Good Father

"A legend, Georgia! One of the most exceptional people I'll ever be privileged to know." Papa was always happy, but this evening at supper he was glowing.

"A Catholic."

"Indeed, and he lives his religion day and night, year in and year—"

"—Being Catholic isn't a religion," Mother snorted. "It's a disease!"

"Dear, I'd happily change my faith to do what that man does for children."

Mother opened her mouth with a reproving "Tch!" and gasped. She said nothing, but pursed her lips in disgust, inspected the kitchen ceiling.

"What does Father Flanagan do for children?" I wanted to know.

"Gives a home to boys who don't have any."

"Boys." She was disappointed. "Where are their Mothers and Papas?"

"They don't have any, sweetheart. Or their parents have so many other worries that they can't help their sons."

"Oh." The six-year-old could not imagine it.

"He borrowed ninety dollars—oh, fifteen years back, rented a house in town that he turned into a hostel for homeless youngsters—uh, boys."

"Thugs, a lot of them," Georgia announced, "and I'll bet you a sweet penny he's never paid back one red cent."

"Georgia," Papa chided mildly, "he's a great man—admit it!"

Mother's voiced softened. "I just can't see any Nebraska Catholic as a hero."

"Would you be more impressed if I told you that Father Flanagan came from Ireland, that he took part of his education in Rome and Austria?"

Mother shrugged, raised her eyebrows. "So he's educated. But he uses people. . . . Look at you-–a good Baptist minister trying to get money donated to hang onto that Overlook place he's building west of town—not even a Baptist organization!"

"The Lord's work is the Lord's work—regardless of what hat's worn by the laborer."

"But two whole years with him, Adolph!"

"The two most useful of my life so far."

"Useful or used!" Mother shrugged. "And why on earth are you taking our six-year-old daughter—"

Papa was smiling at me. "Guess I've talked about her so much, Father wants to meet—"

"—Adolph! Stop calling him 'Father'!"

"Out of habit, Dear. 'Edward' doesn't come easy."

Mother's eyes inspected the ceiling. "There's only one Father." Then, "Does this *man* call you 'Reverend Morse'?"

"Of course not. Phyl will enjoy at least the livestock on the farm, tomorrow."

"You keep an eye out! Don't blow off on some windy project and forget her."

"She'll keep an eye on *me*. Right, Honey?"

I nodded. Papa and I had an understanding that I'd re-mind him when I was with him. Papa did sometimes forget me, even though he loved me. Once, he left me playing in the primary classroom down in the church basement while he varnished a communion table. Then he finished and took the streetcar home. Mother had to drive all the way to church to get me, after she returned from teaching school that day. Papa and I thought the whole thing was funny, particularly since I didn't even known I'd been left. But Mother hadn't laughed.

He'd forgotten me other times, too. But those were our secrets.

Papa didn't drive a car. He was red-green color blind and a little absent-minded. He couldn't remember whether it was the top light or the bottom one that was red. He tended to become so enmeshed in his labyrinth of thought (so Mother had explained to me) that he went right through stop signs and ran into stationary objects like posts and parked cars. Still— and Mother had also told me this—Papa spoke, read and wrote five languages, had a college degree even before he attended the Baptist seminary, and was a perfect human being in spite of how exasperating he was to Mother.

I sat up proudly beside Papa on the woven fiber seat of the streetcar, that next morning, and was glad that Papa never drove. I loved to have people see us together. People who were strangers to me came up often to greet him on streetcars like this and on buses and even on the sidewalk. They'd visit and sometimes talk to me, and then would shake his hand before leaving.

Here on this streetcar that some people called a trolley, I

also enjoyed the lurch of the machine and the clang-clanging of bells at every stop, and the wheezing doors.

But the best about being here with Papa was that when all the seats got full, I could climb onto his lap. Then we were close enough to hear each other talk over the noise of those iron wheels. With so many people riding today, it was not long before Papa reached across and swung me onto his knees. I smelled the good pipe tobacco from the inner pocket of his suit.

"Father Flanagan really wants to see me?" I knew the answer, but I wanted Papa to say it again. Both of my arms were around his neck, and I was looking up at the under part of his chin where his razor didn't get every single whisker.

"Indeed he does! Remember, he sees very few little girls in his line of work."

I nod. "Just lots of ugly boys."

"Boys're nice, too—though I'd not trade you off for a car-load of them."

I gave him a bear hug. "I love you more than anything."

His arms went under mine as he held me up to face him. "More than a dollar?"

"More than a dime." Here was the rhyming game I loved to play with him!

"More than a scholar?"

"More all the time!"

"More than a pocket?"

"More than a nickel!"

"More than a locket?"

"More than a pickle?"

I just looked at him. I couldn't think of another fun word. My mind was blank.

Both of us laughed, and I hugged him again, even though he'd won the game. No one else in the whole world had such a papa!

Both of us laughed, and I hugged him again, even though he'd won the game. No one ⌣ the whole world had such a papa!

"Sure, it's the colleen, is it?" Edward Flanagan grinned, squatted down with robes billowing out, then settling into a black puddle around him. He opened his arms wide to me, nodded his head. "Come on, then, and let's have a look at you."

I was always drawn to any friend of Papa, but I hesitated to go to this one. He had been as tall as Papa before he stooped down, and he had the same laugh wrinkles beside sparkling eyes. He seemed younger—or maybe he just shaved more carefully, I decided, and didn't get involved with practicing his next sermon as Papa did, when he got in front of the bathroom mirror.

But this "Father" was wearing a long black *dress!* And he was wearing beads that hung at his side, not around his neck. I'd never seen a man wear beads at all.

I walked toward him slowly. His arms grasped me, and he swooped me up with him when he stood. "And where would a Roosian get that pale gossamer hair, I'd be liking to know?"

I had to giggle. He had rolled his *r* especially on "Roosian," and I practiced the sound, enjoying the tickle on my tongue.

"A charmer," he told Papa in a hearty voice. Then to me, "Our Sister Ignatius has volunteered to take you touring—see?" He released the arm supporting my back to point. "That wicked-looking witch wearing another black gown!"

"Father!" protested a woman's voice.

Now I noticed for the first time a large woman nearby who was also wearing a long black dress and carrying beads at her side. Her bosom bounced when she chuckled, as she was

21

doing now. But yes, she could put on a pointy hat and be a Halloween witch. But sister? She wasn't *my* sister. I didn't have a sister.

Father Flanagan tossed me high into the air, caught me, then placed me gently on the ground. "Sure, and you run off with Sister now. But if she gives you trouble, you come and find me!"

I looked up to ask the question I'd privately planned. "Will I be able to ride horseback? I mean, do Catholics ride horses?"

This father who wasn't *my* father threw his head back to laugh, slapped Papa on the back, then lowered himself to where his face was once more level with mine. "They ride 'em almost as well as Protestants!" Then in a mock whisper that I knew everyone could hear, he said, "You get Sister Ignatius to rustle up a horse for you—" he glanced up at Papa, who nodded—"and if she doesn't, then you ride *her* pick-a-back all the way to lunch and back!"

As I moved shyly away with the still-chortling "sister," I heard that other Father tell ⌣ Why create Boys Town when girls are so much prettier?"

"Those Catholics all look like other boys," I told Papa in the streetcar when we were going home. "I didn't see a single thug."

Papa laughed. "More Jews and Protestants than Catholics live at Overlook, right at the moment," he told me, "and they all look alike."

"But Mother says—"

"—Hush!" He placed a hand across my mouth. "You

observe for yourself, as the years go by, and then decide."

But I really had to know something, so I persisted. "Mother says I may marry a Negro or a Chinaman or even a bright green Martian, so long as we love each other. But I'm not to marry a Catholic. Why?"

Papa shook his head and sighed. "I honestly don't know where Georgia gets her ideas—from *her* mother? My thoughts on the subject are entirely different. But this is something you need to decide for yourself."

Unfortunately, Papa died before I was ten, long before I made any decision about Catholics—a decision much delayed because— thinking all adult Catholics wore long black dresses with jewelry hanging at their sides—I couldn't spot any.

3

The Contest

He was my favorite cousin Bill, and I was Phyl. So our names rhymed, but there our affinity seemed to cease. We argued about everything. Whether or not that puffy cloud above would produce a summer shower. How many coats of paint were on the barn. Who could sing loudest or longest or closest to the tune. Whether we'd have a hot or cold supper that summer evening. All matters sparked debate.

On one substantial issue, though, we had agreed. At five o'clock on this very afternoon, our two beloved pet rabbits would race. Soon after my mother and I had arrived here to visit in late spring, Bill's daddy—Uncle Pete to me—had gifted Bill and me with two part-grown but biddable cottontails. My uncle had rescued them after accidentally plowing up their field nest with his tractor. And then he had walked up from the barn, that late afternoon, and withdrawn from each overall pocket a furry kit, handing one to each of us.

Gender unknown, Bill and I named them for two beloved uncles, he "Fred" and I "Henry." What presents! A pet of our very own to feed and cuddle, and we'd been at it all summer, so far about six weeks—plus here was a whole new universe for contention. Each of us, naturally, was certain that our own rabbit was superior in every way.

We loved each other, my cousin Bill and I—always had and always would—but as youngsters were forever in competition. To borrow from the old story, Bill was the country mouse, I the city one. We were on Bill's turf this summer, my schoolmarm Mother and I, and I loved being on the Kansas farm with Aunt Margaret, Uncle Pete, even spoiled toddler Carol—and especially with Bill.

He of course was faster replacing halter with bridle when we got ready to ride the unbelievably patient plow-horses Larry (Bill's) and Pearl (mine). And Bill could hit the pail every single time, when we took turns milking a cow. But Bill was always open-mouthed and bug-eyed when he with his family visited "the big city" where I lived—all those people! And I, even very young, could navigate for us on buses and trolleys in Omaha to get to the swimming pool at Peony Park or a movie theater downtown or the roller rink . . . and then home again.

He and I were both four years old, this summer, but I was more four than he, being nine months older. I was also a good bit taller than he. And more substantially built, as well, a condition which lost luster in subsequent years.

"You don't like rutabaga," Bill told me.

I couldn't argue about that.

"Or even spinach," he went on.

I tried to keep my nose from wrinkling.

"And that's why my Fred is going to beat your Henry in the race."

I had no ready response because I was trying to figure out how the speed of a rabbit was conditioned by the diet of its mistress. But I stayed silent. After all, Bill was my smartest cousin.

"And *because* I eat lots of vegetables and fruit," Bill continued, "I'm going to grow taller and stronger than you." He let that pronouncement sink in before adding, "And also *older.*"

Was that even possible? I hadn't lived enough years to know the answer.

No doubt about it, though, I was basically a carnivore, looking back, not a vegetarian. Not even close. I spent all except our Kansas summer times in South Omaha, Nebraska, a U.S. stockyard and meat packing center (Swift, Armour and Cudahy) with serious competition only from Chicago in those mid-years of the economically depressed 1930s. Hamburger or t-bone, bacon or ham—here were the nuclei around which meals were built.

Not rutabaga, thank goodness.

Bill's back yard was fair sized, the laterals marked indistinctly by open woodland but with a rickety fence along the far side, perhaps fifteen yards away from our starting point on the porch steps. That fence was something visible that we both agreed would be the goal. Whichever bunny got there first, Fred or Henry, would be the winner. Simple, evident, and for once no room for argument.

Both of us kept a close watch that afternoon on the clock which hung on the kitchen wall, over by the big black iron stove. I have no recollection of how we arrived on and agreed that five o'clock was the "proper time" for the race so long awaited and so frequently discussed—and with probable result so often argued. I certainly don't remember our ever setting and abiding by a scheduled time for any of our many other activities and adventures together, those previous or subsequent.

But there we were, a bit before five o'clock and huddled on the back porch steps, Bill stroking Fred's ears and I rubbing Henry's belly while I murmured to him that he must run *fast.*

Then we two cousins both squatted down, put our fluffy pets on the ground while gently restraining them as we prepared to give the signal. . . .

"One-two-three-GO!" we said together as we released the rabbits.

Fred took a couple of hops forward, bit off and munched a bit of grass browned by the August sun, then headed in a leisurely manner for the woodland on our left. My Henry seemed not to be hungry, but he too bounced forward twice before turning to the right and making a casual exit into the trees on *that* side.

I looked at Bill, and he looked at me, both of us realizing at once that our pets had not *understood.* Or perhaps they did grasp our plan but *disagreed.*

Nor did either of us follow after in an attempt to recover the soft little creatures we had fed and watered and petted for weeks. Instead, we turned to each other gape-mouthed, our ears filled with the sound of Uncle Pete's laughter from where he'd been standing on the back porch to observe the Big Race.

Bill and I remained best friends in all the many years to come—even though we saw each other rarely as adults who had selected differing life paths that kept us far apart. Although he continued to pursue a healthy diet, Bill never did get taller than I, nor older. And although I can become enthusiastic over a well-cheesed spinach-and-mushroom pizza, I still dislike rutabaga.

4

. . . .

(Omaha, Nebraska)

Blood Relations

Not long ago—but many decades after the fact—I asked my half-brother what he remembered about our grandfather. Richard is seventeen years older than I and one of three off-spring from my father's first marriage before that wife died in childbirth.

"Well, none of us understood his Russian or German, so we couldn't actually talk. But he played with us—tag outside, hide and seek in the house!—and I remember his trotting me on his knee when I was very young, his teaching us to sing Christmas carols in German or Russian—he always loved his grandchildren."

I didn't respond at the time, but I was incredulous that we spoke of the same man.

In the mid-Thirties, when what would someday be referred to as The Great Depression was well underway, and before such a thing as Social Security became more than a dream, the brothers and sisters of my father were no longer able to contribute money for the monthly upkeep of their parents. My mother was a teacher being paid mostly with an I.O.U. (Subsequently paid off!) and a Voucher for the grocery store of her choice (O.P. Skaggs, as I recall), and my father was a minister paid almost entirely by homegrown potatoes and jars of jam. But we had food enough for five. No one at our house in this new arrangement during these bleak days was going to starve. So we went to live with Grandma and Grandpa in their big white house. . . .

A five-year-old has neither the vocabulary to win an argument nor the bulk to win a fight. Thus, most youngsters grow up with aggression—wrath unvented and frustration unresolved.

Dr. Freud noted and prospered from this fact.

But I don't have this problem. No childhood-induced umbrage plagues me, no subconscious anger surfaces at unexpected moments. And this consummate condition I owe almost entirely to the paternal grandfather whom I queried my brother about. During those for him senescent years of seventy-nine through eighty-one, and for me formative years of four through six, Grandpa and I vented our respective wraths, massaged our frustrations and flared our furies to a fare-thee-well.

I realize in retrospect that we were probably well matched—I the young and inexperienced only child in the home; he in his eighties and (likely) suffering from dementia.

So different our backgrounds! Grandpa, a legend in the lofty realm of adults in community, neighborhood and family. A shopkeeper in Russia during the latter decades of the Nineteenth Century, Grandpa had watched the Czar become difficult about prosperous Anabaptist German communities even as the Russian people became difficult about the Czar. So Grandpa had in 1892 taken Grandma and my seven-year-old father to the Land of Opportunity.

Grandpa fought his way out of Veronish in Russia onto a ship to New York. Then battled a route from the East Coast

29

across the American plains to homestead in the northwest corner of Nebraska. There, he experienced drought, prairie fire, clouds of ravenous insects and sometimes unfriendly Native Americans to skirmish up not only a living for his burgeoning family but also funds sufficient to move to the big city of Omaha by the time his four sons and two daughters were ready for higher education.

Grandpa, then, was a scrapper with dimensions of length and breadth. His history of combat dated back to a time when success in the fray meant survival. Grandpa had learned not ever to let go. He thrived on confrontation and flourished through persistence. And I was his present problem! I perceive all this now but not then.

A frequently recounted family story dates back to a time when the family left their northwest Nebraska homestead to find formal schooling for their adolescent sons. They first arrived during the early 1920's in South Omaha, then a refuge for immigrants willing to work in the stockyards and packing houses clustered there. Grandpa got himself lost somewhere downtown and telephoned home for the boys to come and get him.

Gustaf Adolph, my papa and his eldest son, asked, "Where are you?"

"If I knew where I was," Grandpa retorted in wrathful Russian, "I wouldn't be lost!" And he slammed down the receiver.

After the harsh austerity of the Depression subsided with the outbreak of World War II in Europe, we moved back home. But when the U.S. became involved in that war, government officials—so the story goes—learned my grandfather was *pro*-German. Several men interviewed the old man there at the house. They went on to talk to neighbors and some other acquaintances. And they did not interne him, but left him right there in his big white Victorian house in South Omaha, Nebraska. They had decided his influence was such that he could best serve the Allied Cause by remaining at large in the community and aligned with the enemy.

Best defined in my recollection are nearly two years of unmitigated struggle. Grandfather vs. granddaughter. He had the edge in experience and I suppose credibility, should our combat surface. But I was possibly more creative, certainly less accurate. He used a rifle, I a shotgun.

What kind of kid I was Before Grandpa, I don't know. Like most small fry when you really get to know them, I was probably convinced that all the planets circled *me;* and I was therefore lovable mostly to my parents. Nor was I charmed by the company of peers.

For example, the girl up the street who was my age liked playing with dolls and dressing up in high heels and wearing her big sister's makeup—all of which gives you an idea of the kind of person *she* was. And the flame-haired boy next door whose mother made superior lemonade even in winter was a passable playmate for a limited time—the limit being soon after lemonade was served.

So . . . around the middle of The Depression, about 1935, when the aunts and uncles were temporarily unable to contribute each month toward support of the family patriarch and matriarch, during these days pre-dating Social Security, my parents rented out our own home and moved us into the big old South Omaha Victorian with Grandpa and Grandma. Mother and Papa at least had jobs. On the very day we moved in, Grandpa must have identified me as an antagonist. He *knew* immediately, I'm certain; but the patient man waited to make his moves.

At home, Grandpa spoke Russian to Grandma and Papa, spoke German to Mother and those visiting family or friends to whom he spoke at all. But he never, ever spoke one word to me. After Grandma preceded him in death by a few years, the family was astonished to discover he spoke English better than she ever had.

I remember Grandpa as slim and bald and energetic, always prefaced by an untidy mustache that expressed his frequent disapproval with twitches and the angle at which it was held. His domain was the outdoors—the front and side lawns, the fruit trees and garden in the rear yard, and along the back fence his ramshackle tool shed—a structure which included boards which did not always meet but nevertheless had a bolt lock inside the warped door.

And it was Grandpa who cared for the yard and house exterior, who took responsibility for cleaning and rotating screen and storm windows on the forty-three apertures in vertical walls which permitted a view of our vigorous Nebraska seasons.

What I did to engender initial disfavor, I don't remember. Looking back, a dozen early transgressions come to mind— any of which would have been sufficient to ignite his ready ire. Certainly I walked on freshly-hosed walkways. I doubtless tracked mud—I was nearly five years old. I do remember that some bluejays nesting in the front yard maple once swooped down to peck at his glistening pate as he walked directly below. I snickered. His scowl communicated displeasure with my reaction, but I nevertheless broke into laughter. I remember thinking that even the jays knew how grouchy the man was.

But all in all, I'm certain I ran when I should have walked, spoke when I should have been silent, trod in areas sacrosanct. Grandpa was no longer accustomed to three-foot-high kidlets in his household, and of me he disapproved thoroughly.

The formal start to our enmity included a period of testing, observing reactions, setting up boundaries. As it turned out, we had rules, Grandpa and I. Tacit but clearly understood. Even grim games must have regulations. That ours were unspoken weakened their power not at all. *We never actually **touched** each other, and we never told.* This latter was violated by him, finally; but by that time the grim game was out of hand.

From my earliest recollection, Mother always made it clear to me that if I chose to do battle, I must handle the problem entirely by myself. *And you don't ever tattle!* She was after all a school teacher—and she *hated* tattling. As I learned later, she believed that the human brain and a civil tongue were what was required to avoid serious confrontation. But Mother had evolved from gentler folk than her father-in-law. My papa had very likely never had so much as an argument with anyone in his entire life, so mellow was his demeanor, so mild his presence.

Grandpa and I had those two checks, then—*don't touch and don't tell.* I, at least, abided by them throughout the time we lived together, and I still get a glimmer of pride from that fact. In retrospect, it seems necessary for Grandpa to finally break the rules, probably as a means to insure our mutual longevity. We played rough.

Knowing well that my presence was an irritant, I followed Grandpa outdoors like his own shadow on a sunny day. I stood to stare. I hunkered down for long-term vigilance. I peered through the cobwebby tool shed window when he retreated within to sharpen a tool or locate the proper screwdriver to tighten hinges on the back door of the house. He would flare his fingers at me, for that one window provided his only illumination in the shed. And I would move slightly, for my parents had taught me to obey adults; but I would continue to observe.

Restraint relaxed as we found ourselves in relatively full knowledge of the enemy. I had a new, swirly blue dress with white polka dots one could *feel* with one's fingers—called a "dotted swiss" in those days—which I liked and wore on every possible occasion.

It disappeared. I searched my closet, the clothes hampers, the ironing basket, even the edges of the yard where wind might have blown it from the clothesline. Some weeks later, while trying to retrieve the cat, I found this dress plus some other items of my clothing rolled up and irretrievably mildewed on a high dirt ledge in the corner of the crawl space in an unfinished part of the cellar. The very next Saturday morning, I saw Grandpa removing items of my damp clothing from the line where Mother had hung them only minutes before. *Don't tattle, just get even!*

My revenge was to pick and distribute among neighbors the fruit from his only apple tree. I would wait until he was engrossed in some project, then take the ripening Pippins, a dozen or so at a time in a brown grocery bag. I would walk from house to house to make my donations. Being a good climber and doggedly persistent, I managed to divest the tree of apples within a week.

It never did occur to me that the members of our family counted on eating those apples. Nor did I ever realize, while busily engaged in dreaming up and doing destruction, that I was wounding others as well as Grandpa. Our at-first-petty aggressions flourished. He had far better accuracy, I can see now, where my retaliations tended to affect everyone. Certainly, that was not my conscious aim.

Our quietly escalating combat did not really hit full stride until the second and last year we were in the big house. When I came home from kindergarten one afternoon, I was astonished to see my bedroom upstairs had been emptied. Only window curtains remained. The closet was bare, too, and my footsteps echoed in the stark room. The chest of drawers was easy: it stood in the upstairs bathroom full of neatly folded towels and washcloths.

Parts of my twin bed were in various closets and lurking behind bureaus and in the shadows of some always-open doors. I finally got the mattress rolled down the hall after extricating it from the top shelf of the massive linen closet. I spied and reclaimed my straight-backed chair from the dining room downstairs. The major task of searching out clothing and toys took me until Mother and Papa returned from work and it was time for dinner. The attic and the cellar turned up major caches, but with fair portions stowed among drawers and closets throughout the other five bedrooms upstairs. I shall never know whether everything was retrieved.

Although most of our sorties took place more or less invisibly out-of-doors after that incident, my grandmother must have observed at least the bedroom clearing. But she was a well-disciplined Northeast European woman, a servant to her husband. She could not have intervened, and somehow it never occurred to me she might.

It was several days, that early spring, before satisfactory reprisal presented itself. Something simple and diabolical—and with characteristically poor aim. Grandpa's garden had just begun to show bright green sprouts in row on row, the fading seed packets with still-recognizable pictures punctured by sticks at one end of each new section.

Down those rows I went. Celery, onions, radishes, carrots, beans, even freshly-transplanted tomatoes. I toed out and tossed willy-nilly everything but the beets. Grandpa didn't like beets, but the family insisted he cultivate them for borscht and pickles.

Of course Grandpa replanted, for it was still early in the season, and I left the new garden alone. But we were considerably later than our neighbors to enjoy fresh vegetables that year.

During the summer before we moved into the Victorian and I started kindergarten at Corrigan, while my folks and I were visiting Mother's relatives in rural Kansas, I had managed to smash the middle finger of my right hand. We sought medical service tardily, and even then aid was mediocre, a rural approach. By the time we returned to Omaha at vacation's end, I had serious infection which continued for years. The finger was saved, but I will always write with my left hand.

That finger with its seeping wrappers, along with its proclivity for further injury, was an ongoing annoyance for me and an anxiety for my parents; but it represented a prime target for Grandpa. The finger was a blemish on my existence, I thought then: the repeated, often painful trips to the doctor, the continual warnings against bumping and re-injuring it, against getting it dirty or wet, against *using* it generally.

Worst was my vulnerability. As time passed, this one digit became the focal point in my grandfather's efforts. He was canny, almost playful. In the front yard, he would throw the newspaper at me, not toss it, so I could take it into the house. It always came to my right side and I would instinctively reach out either to protect myself or try to snatch it mid-air—yes, with my right hand. My place at the table was to Grandpa's left. He would pass me a hot serving dish, letting go prematurely so I must grasp it with the near hand or else spill it.

But he was at his best with doors. He must have waited many minutes by the side yard entrance to assure that it would suddenly, mysteriously swing out just as I approached, would bang "accidentally" against the shrouded finger. And each time, Grandpa would march out and pass me stolidly with no glance to left or right.

Then would follow the agonizing trip to the doctor once again for blood stoppage and disinfecting, the long-familiar warnings and exhortations. I doubt Grandpa ever considered his activity in combination with my own clumsy accidents might actually cause me to lose that finger. But neither octogenarians nor five-year-olds have much regard for consequences.

I didn't know Grandpa was in his rickety tool shed when I started in for a hammer. Perhaps he had been waiting for me, but I think probably not, as I did not ordinarily dare to enter his sanctuary. The whole setup, from his viewpoint, was more likely felicitous happenstance. For when my right hand pushed open the door, a right hand complete with bandaged monstrosity splinted straight out from the palm, the rickety shed door suddenly closed on it. Hard. Very hard. The finger was caught, and I could not extract it. I tugged and pulled and floundered. Then I heard the bolt slide into place on the other side.

I shouted at Grandpa to open the door, told him my finger was caught—"Just look and see!" I cried and pleaded and even threatened to tell. But it must have been a full five minutes which seemed like hours before the bolt came away and pressure was released. Grandpa stalked past me looking straight ahead. He had a fine excuse, should it come to that: he spoke no English.

That time, I was in the hospital for two days. Neither Mother nor Papa could understand how my "catching it in a door" could break even the splint. I exited on my sixth birthday with a cast on my whole hand and a chorus of admonitions to Please Be Very Careful This Time.

I was. You cannot imagine a more careful child. I was cautious, even paranoid. And I was waiting. . . .

But not for long. It took only a few weeks before the perfect opportunity presented itself. I came home from school one sunny but brisk afternoon in early October and beheld an exceptional sight along the side of the house. Lining the broad lawn lay what seemed to be acres of freshly-polished, sparkling storm windows and doors. Their shiny faces beamed up at the mid-afternoon sun.

Upstairs in the closet, I dug around for my high-top snow boots from last winter. They were sufficiently sturdy but no longer fit over my shoes. In those days, snow boots were called "galoshes," and everyone's shoes went inside. I removed my shoes and put on some layers of Papa's wool socks so the footwear would stay on as I marched down the stairs and out the side door at the top of the cellar steps.

I began at the beginning, like Alice in Wonderland, and did not stop until the end. I stepped carefully and methodically down onto the center of each pane. A few small rectangles on the doors resisted at first but succumbed to sharp heel jabs. The glass in forty-three windows having at least two panes each perished on that afternoon in a grim game of stylized hopscotch. Plus three doors having many sections of glass.

Well into the task I had set for myself, Grandpa appeared. He stood expressionless, for once not even scowling, as he observed my progress through the last ten or so windows. Then he disappeared.

Breathless and triumphant, I went around to the front of the house to wait for my parents. But Grandpa was there. He had dragged a porch rocker down to the walkway just inside our gate, blocking the path. He was smoking a cigar, something he did only when agitated, but that was his only show of emotion. He sat up very straight, rocking and facing the street. Peculiar, I thought. I couldn't remember his ever doing that before.

My mother drove up in our old black Ford, and we waved to each other, I from the safety of the front porch. She turned when she got out to pick up a couple of sacks of groceries, then started for the house, stopped when she saw Grandpa, moved forward uncertainly.

He didn't say anything to her until she was inside the gate. Then he got up and pushed the rocker to the side, took the sacks from her—an uncharacteristic courtesy—and started speaking in rapid-fire German. He kept dipping his head sideways in my direction, walked backward to lead her around the corner of the porch to the side yard.

They were there for a long time. I heard the old man switch over to vehement Russian, listened to my mother's voice rising first in German, next in English. Then both voices subsided, and I heard nothing.

That old man wasn't playing fair. I felt betrayed. He wasn't supposed to *tell!* I wouldn't have. I never did. I recall a hollow feeling of disorientation—a sense of violation. But I remember no remorse at all.

I went indoors quietly and set the table for dinner. Late. Usually, this chore was done before Mother and Papa arrived so we could talk a little or play a short game. Never mind, I'd been busy.

Dinner seemed strained that evening. I kept trying to catch Mother's eye; but although she spoke to me, "Please pass the green beans, Phyllis," I couldn't hold her gaze. Something was going to happen. Perhaps I should explain that Mother was the disciplinarian in my family. Papa was perfect, and it never occurred to him that anyone else might not be. Day-to-day dalliances were unobserved by him, unworthy of regard. Those few incidents such as this one surely was, events which jarred his world and thereby came to his attention, he would accept serenely while working out the motivation. Failure to find an explanation, he always told me, was due to limitation on the part of the observer. An unusual clergyman, my papa.

Mother, however, was a no-nonsense fifth grade teacher who expected her only chick to encompass all of the virtues of all of her students over all of the years she had taught. In most instances, she paddled first and asked questions later. She brooked no disobedience, no insubordination . . . and of course I learned early to operate underground, to be silent and sneaky.

Tattling was not acceptable. Besides, Grandpa and I had this unspoken agreement. I'm sure neither of my parents had any idea of the scope to their daughter's battle—not *ever*.

For totally different reasons, neither of my parents were people one could burden willy-nilly with one's troubles, although both were kind and loving in their ways. I never asked Mother about this period as an adult in later years—perhaps because I had so many questions about other matters—but I am certain the restraint she showed where Grandpa and I were concerned must have stemmed from intuitive knowledge of a double-sided blade at work.

Had she ever questioned me to get my view on the misadventures of that period, I know I would not have divulged anything. I didn't understand what was happening then—nor do I fully understand now. Probably, at the time, I possessed neither the concepts nor the language to express myself on the subject.

But as years passed and I got a better handle on what is and is not usual in this life, I became certain—as I remain today!—that neither Mother nor Papa had any inkling of the scope of our combat, Grandpa's and mine. I also know those two years were difficult ones for Mother, as well. Perhaps, subconsciously, she even approved of what little she perceived of her daughter's petty vengeances. Mother had a different *Bible* verse applicable to most situations. One repeated frequently during our stay with the in-laws was "This too shall pass."

On the evening of the demise of the storm windows, Papa turned on the big yard light we rarely used because of the electricity it consumed. Mother sent me upstairs for a measuring tape from the sewing machine, I recall, and for paper and pencil from the desk in the corner of their bedroom. Long past my bedtime—and on a school night, too!—she and Papa and I were outside measuring for new glass.

No spanking or scolding ever came. But sometime during that evening activity, the pleasure in my deviltry diminished. This thing big people called *Depression* meant money was scarce. And even in my selfish, insulated world, I realized my parents and not Grandpa were going to pay for replacing the glass I had smashed. It turned out to be a very long evening, and I held my side of the tape measure carefully without wriggling and without letting it slip and without having to be told to move on to the next skeleton frame in the wreckage, Papa calling out the figures and Mother writing them down.

That was the end of my revenge. The rancor continued, but Grandpa had to play the game all by himself. I went into a straight defensive pattern for the duration of our stay at the Victorian, a strategy which has in fact come naturally to me ever since—in chess, at cocktail parties in the male-dominated profession I entered as an adult. Even today, my sins tend to be omissive rather than commissive (no less *sinful,* of course).

I am not sure Grandpa ever noticed the change. That Christmas, I spent a dime of my Christmas-shopping dollar on a yo-yo for him in his favorite black color—at least, that's the color he always wore. I specially asked the Kresge clerk for a box to fit it, and then I wrapped it carefully if not lovingly, curled the crinkly strips of paper with a scissor blade and placed the package on a branch at tree center so it wouldn't look so small. It was, in fact, just below another branch with another small package, this one without paper or ribbon, which bore a plain white card with strange script.

Early on Christmas morning, Grandpa received and opened his present from me fairly soon, stiffly tried to operate the toy after I and then Papa showed him how, finally sat holding it in his lap, the string still around his finger, the lines in his stern face slightly softened, his eyes on me. When the unribboned package went to my father for his sonorous proclamation of recipient and giver, he studied the white card a moment, then announced that the box was for me from Grandpa. Even Grandma was surprised, because Grandpa never gave gifts to anyone. Everybody paused while I tore off the paper and opened the box.

Inside was . . . clay? Spoiled clay, I guessed from the bad smell. Probably from being closed up so long and on the tree near lights. The substance was smoothed level with the top of the box, but not wrapped in cellophane like the clay at school.

Mother reached over for the gift, examined it a moment, lifted it to her nostrils, then stiffened. She took the boxtop from me as she closed the box and stood up in one movement and stalked from the room. Protesting, I followed her to the cellar door where she fumbled with the bolt. To my agitated questions, she would only shake her head, lips pursed in a determined way she had which warned me not to push too far. She had trouble with the sliding bolt because, I noticed, her hand seemed to be shaking. When the door opened at last, she descended the steps and moved straightaway to our coal furnace.

The heavy door opened to reveal a fiery maw. I risked her wrath to complain again—after all, it was *my* present, wasn't it? She threw box and contents far back into the flame, clanged the door shut and returned to the stairs. I saw moisture glistening in her eyes, and was alarmed until I realized it must be from the furnace heat when she had the door open. No adult I knew ever cried.

At the top of the stairs, Mother slid the bolt home, then turned to me and yes, definitely, what looked like tears fogged her eyes, one droplet actually sliding down her cheek. Suddenly, she lifted me up and hugged me, leaving me breathless and surprised. No one in my family, and least of all my mother, was demonstrative.

"Sorry, Phyllis. You get your new things and bring them up to Mother and Papa's room. We'll play some games."

I turned to obey but was confused. We played games as a family at the small table in the kitchen. Alone, I was allowed to play in a corner of the living room near the fireplace, in the big entry hall near the closet with its box of toys, or else up in my room—not anywhere else in the house. Well, but today was Christmas, so that must be it.

I heard arguing as I returned to the living room. Grandma's usually mild voice was several tones higher than usual, her Russian uncharacteristically fast-paced and loud. Papa looked agitated. When Grandma saw me, she fell silent. I stared at Grandpa. He was rocking back and forth in front of the fireplace, the yo-yo string ludicrously tangled around his fingers, and laughing. I had not ever heard Grandpa laugh. His face was contorted and his eyes glittered.

Grandma asked him in Russian what was clearly a question, but he ignored her, just stared into the hearth fire where logs were crackling in accompaniment to his rusty guffaws.

Papa stood up. "And what can I do for my favorite little girl?" he asked too heartily.

I studied his face. "Mother said I should take my things up to—up to *your* room. She said we might play. Maybe my new game?"

"That's right!" Papa agreed as he scooped up my stack of Christmas loot. "That's exactly what we'll do!" I continued to watch his face. His always pleasant features seemed to be frozen.

When I began to collect wrappings to discard, Grandma stopped me. "You play, already," she told me in her uncertain English. Her wrinkled hand turned my face up, and she kissed me softly on the forehead. "I throw wrappers in fire," she added, and gave me a little push in the direction Papa had taken.

As I started up the steps, I heard her voice begin again, speaking rapid Russian, pausing as if to wait for an answer, then starting in once more.

And Grandpa kept right on laughing.

A few weeks later on a frigid Saturday in mid-January, the telephone rang during breakfast. It was for Papa, and after he listened for a few seconds, he started speaking German, something about driving to Lincoln today. Returning to the table, he explained that his youngest sister was in the capital city without any money. Traveling home from school by train, she was now stranded by snowdrifts that blocked further progress. Public transport had halted as a blizzard moved in. Papa and Mother were to go by auto and pick her up.

This was my jolly Aunt Sophie, and I wanted to ride along.

But no. Mother said the roads were uncertain—they planned to take blankets with them, in case they got stuck. She reminded me about how restless I got when we traveled long distances. "With these roads, we'll likely be in the car all day, there and back. That's if we get through at all."

It was decided that I would stay home and help Grandma make cookies especially for Aunt Sophie. And actually, the day was pleasant enough, cozy inside with the wind howling around the house. The kitchen was warm and spicy. Besides, I had a new kitten I had found half dead with cold and lying beside a snowdrift. One ear had been frozen flat and was lifeless still. The cat needed me to feed and take care of it. Grandma made a special concession and let me bring it upstairs from the basement to a box we fixed in the kitchen under the four-legged oven stove in which we baked cookies throughout the brief light of that day.

Grandma held back supper for more than an hour before Papa's voice came through on the phone. They had swung over to Prairie Home, on their way back from Lincoln, to check that Uncle Al and Aunt Minnie were all right in the storm. They were, but the highway home was drifted high and impassable. Everyone would stay the night in this tiny town, then follow snow plows to Omaha tomorrow in the light of day.

Although I was usually alone with Grandma and Grandpa around school hours during the day, I could not remember ever spending a night without at least one of my parents in the house. We had a silent, half-cold meal, and then Grandpa went to the cellar to bank the furnace for the night. It was already past my bedtime, but no one paid attention. When Grandpa came upstairs, he renewed the fire in the fireplace, sat in his rocker and started reading the German periodicals to which he subscribed. All exactly as he did every evening, except everything was happening later, and Papa wasn't sitting nearby and reading his books.

Grandma and I washed up dishes and pans just as usual, only Mother wasn't there to chatter back and forth in English and German. Grandma complimented me on drying the drinking glasses to a shine, I remember, and then gave me a cookie. Mother would never have let me have anything to eat after supper, no matter what. Still, I wished she were here. Then, Grandma snapped off the kitchen light and went upstairs, also as usual. I played in the front hallway with the kitten for a while.

The wind had risen to a wild roar, or perhaps I noticed it more in the otherwise silent house. The gale tried to blast its way through doors and windows, then shrieked annoyance ever louder over not being able to invade our house completely. A draft came around the front door, nevertheless. And chill came through edges of the windows in spite of Grandpa's double panes.

I rummaged in the hall closet until I found my father's raggedy yard sweater. It was comforting—woolly and snug, redolent of Papa himself. Later, I found myself drifting off and decided it was time to put the cat back into the cellar and go to bed even though no one was going to tell me to. Grandpa had forgotten to bolt the cellar door, and it was easy to flick the light switch and carry the striped ball of fur down to its cardboard box behind the furnace. But on this particular night of storm and wild wind, or perhaps in memory of its day in the warm kitchen, the kitten scrambled out of the nest and beat me to the foot of the steps. There, it sat and mewed.

Just as I stooped to pick it up and return it to its bed, the cellar door closed at the top of the steps, the bolt shot, and the lights snapped off.

"Grandpa! I'm down here!"

No answer.

I stumbled up the steps and pounded on the door. "Grandpa! Grandpa, *here I am!* GRANDMA!"

But the only sound was the shrieking wind.

I kept shouting until I was hoarse. Maybe he would come back, slide the bolt silently and go away. I sat down on the top step to listen. I was swaddled in Papa's sweater and cradling the kitten. I would reach up to try the door every few minutes, but there was no give.

It was cold. The air tasted icy despite the furnace being here, and the blare of wind drowned out most other sound. The single window over the work table whistled and rattled as the gale sought entry. I was glad to have the kitten, glad to hear it purring when I raised the warm little body to my ear, glad to feel it vibrating on my lap, also covered by Papa's sweater, warming my hands as I petted it.

After what seemed a very long time, I caught myself falling forward and knew I had dozed off. My eyes burned, and I had trouble keeping them open in the darkness. I stood up and tried the door once more before feeling my way cautiously back down the steps. A person could fall if she fell asleep up there. A pale luminescence came through the small, high window above the work bench, now that my eyes were accustomed to the dark.

Opening the furnace door, I peered at a weak orange glow nestled at the base of coal lumps inside. Clutching the kitten with my good hand, I put the bandaged hand inside to feel for warmth. Very little. I would have to sit inside the furnace to enjoy much warmth, and I didn't think I should do that.

What I *should* do was build up the fire, as I had many times seen Papa and Grandpa do in the mornings. I would just go get a scuttle full of coal from the bin and stoke up a blaze with the poker always leaning against the furnace. But when I opened the bin door, an icy blast struck me and something hit my foot hard, then squeaked and went scurrying beyond me across the floor. I closed the door quickly, stood very still and thought I could hear rustling on the far, unfinished side of the cellar.

I went back to close the furnace door. No use poking up a blaze without adding fuel. The fire would burn high, then go out completely. I wanted to get off the floor, partly because it was too cold to sit on and partly because of the squeaking creature I had let inside. Too sleepy to sit safely on the steps—well, maybe at the bottom without so far to fall. But then what about the animal from the coal bin? That left the work surface in front of the window. It might be even colder than the floor, though, because of the glass.

I put the kitten up on the counter, talking to it, patting it, then crawled up beside it as I pushed tools and wood scraps aside. Perhaps I could nail boards across the window for warmth—and maybe Grandma would wonder what the pounding was about and come down to investigate. But the scraps were too small; and I knew that a truck could probably drive back and forth through the cellar without anyone in a second-floor bedroom hearing it above the gale outdoors.

Shuddering from the windflow around the frame, I got another idea. Why not just go out the window and over to Martin's house? Never mind how late it was. They had a doorbell I could ring and ring until someone answered. I loved to ring doorbells. I felt all around the frame twice. The window was mounted from outside. Well then. I could use a stick to break the glass and get out. *Both* panes if a storm window was involved. But then I remembered how I had already broken quite a lot of glass, and not so very long ago, either. I was suddenly certain I shouldn't do that.

So I buried my hands in the kitten's fur, snuggled as deeply as possible into Papa's sweater, and waited for morning. I remembered Mother had said at breakfast that the radio in their room had reported seven degrees below zero even with the sun shining. I thought it must by now be at least three hundred degrees below zero. Never before had I given thought to how long night was before morning came. I kept dozing and then waking up with shivers and wondering how much longer it would be. Sometime during the night, I woke up to feel moisture on my hand. The wind must have shifted. Now the blast was coming directly at the window, driving fine bits of snow right through the casing. Keeping the kitten close, I moved over so that I was beside the window instead of in front of it. Now the draft and whistling storm seemed to miss me.

After hours of rearranging the sweater and even the cat to cover whatever parts of me seemed coldest, I came wide awake suddenly to the sound of the bolt shifting in the door above. Just before the overhead bulb brightened, I realized that a dim gray light was coming through the top part of the window, that the rest of it was piled with snow. It seemed slightly warmer, and the wind had died down. It must be morning.

"Grandpa?!" I watched the bony ankles above brown plaid house slippers as they descended the stairway next to me. "You left me down here all night."

He reached the bottom step, started for the furnace. "Grandpa? It was too cold to leave me down here," I scolded.

Even from behind, where I was now, I could usually see his broad mustaches working and estimate his mood from the action of those facial hairs. But nothing. They might as well have belonged to someone else's grandpa.

He opened the furnace door, inspected the glowing bank, stirred it with the poker, reached up to adjust the damper.

"Grandpa?" I was trying to get off the work table, but parts of me were asleep and all of me was stiff.

He went to open the coal bin, withdrew the shovel and filled the scuttle with black lumps.

"I think there might be a family of rats who live in there," I warned him. "Maybe they came in through the chute because of the storm."

Grandpa tipped the scuttle to toss its contents deep into the freshening flames, then stoked a while. He stood the poker in its place, carried the scuttle back to the bin, returned to study the fire in the blackened furnace.

"Grandpa, you shouldn't have left me here last night!"

I edged forward slowly, began to clamber down as silently as possible, for Grandpa could still beat me to the stairway and lock me in again. I willed him not to turn back and see me. It would be easy, now, to slip off the edge and move like a shadow across the cellar floor . . . even to the furnace. And then . . . what?

He was a shriveled old man, grumpy and ugly to everyone, I decided as my feet touched the concrete floor. And he was mean—cruel to me and cruel to Mother, too, he must be. I remembered her tears on Christmas Day, although I still did not know why she had cried.

The kitten was awake under Papa's sweater, disturbed by my movements, had begun a ragged purr. I placed it gently back up onto the work table, petted it, scratched under its chin. I did not want it to mew.

50

Grandpa was probably cruel to Grandma, too, grumpy and ugly and ornery to everyone except maybe Papa. Perhaps he was that way because he was so old, but I didn't think so. Grandma wasn't like that, and neither was my grandmother down in Kansas, and they seemed to be at least as old as Grandpa. This old man was very clever—and very quick, I reminded myself , whenever he wanted to be.

I moved forward, away from the table and across the floor toward the silhouette before the furnace, one soft step and then another. No, I decided, Grandpa was a truly vicious man, through and through. Especially, exceptionally mean. But Papa wasn't, and Grandma wasn't or Mother . . . and I wouldn't be, either. Not now or ever.

I turned back to the stairway. It no longer mattered about sound. He couldn't stop me, and I flew up the steps two at a time, raced through the door and spun around into the entry hall, then on up more steps and down the upstairs hall, not stopping until I was inside my own room with the door closed and me panting against it.

No lock was on my door, but that didn't matter. Grandpa would never actually touch me, and I planned not to leave my bedroom until my parents came back—not for breakfast, not to feed the kitten, not even to go to the bathroom. Maybe it would take all day, or maybe a week or even a month if the snow kept falling. So maybe it would be until Spring. But I would not go out of this room until they came.

I took off only my shoes and the sweater before leaping onto the bed and pulling up the blanket roll from the foot and tucking it in all around. Papa's sweater, I put under my neck and around my face over my ears.

I guessed Grandpa had won the game, or at least he would think he had, even though he was the only one who'd been playing, anymore. My shivering finally ceased before I fell asleep. I remember thinking that everything seemed very different this morning, as if some other little girl had taken the kitten to the cellar last night after getting a cookie from her grandma and playing alone in the entry hall.

Grandpa just didn't matter, anymore. I would ignore him, as everyone else did. And I wasn't a mean person. Maybe I had been worrying about that. For a long time. I felt light and free, free of Grandpa. Free of much.

That was the end. Grandpa's assaults ceased, even if his rancor quite obviously did not. He never did speak directly to me, never until the very day he died at ninety-five, some years after the brand new broom of World War II swept away the Depression. He was a rough teacher, but I learned a lot. Watch Your Backside. Try Not to Start Something You Won't Be Willing to Finish. I also learned something he had known all along—that one can lead a pleasant existence even without the full approbation of every single person around you.

I have thought often, over the years, about our strange and secret relationship. And I have come to the decision that Grandpa and I were deeply involved with each other. We were *friends,* if one can define friendship as Random House does, "attachment through personal regard." We regarded each other a great deal. We (or at least I) took each other into account throughout most waking minutes of those nearly two years, almost up to the day my parents and I moved out of the Victorian, my aunts and uncles once again able to contribute toward their parents' support.

I know Grandpa thrived on the experience, and something of the daily savoring must have vanished from his life after the cellar incident when I stopped "playing" entirely. And I learned something else, too: *walk away early if you find yourself in a contest you cannot win and especially if you know that you are incapable of or unwilling to go the distance.* Grandpa never did thank me for those times. But I thank *him.* Now.

Uncle Charlie & The Tornado

It is about seven decades since 1941 when Uncle Charlie confronted the tornado, but some memories are indelible. I remember being with my relatives on that Friday Fourth of July in North-central Missouri, and I am there at Uncle Charlie's house and at the community picnic under the trees by the Muddy River—and then up on the ballfield where it all happened.

"Where's Uncle Charlie?" I'm standing at his rough slab of a door. I have a chocolate cake on my one arm and a bowl of fruit salad on the other.

"Fishing, honey. He'll bring a big string of fresh-caught buffaloes to the picnic today, just wait and see. Push the door with your elbow."

I do. It opens onto a place the size of Aunt Lois and Uncle Jim's back porch lean-to, maybe twelve feet square. Dirt floor. Two small windows. A cot made up neatly. A two-burner kerosene stove. An old wooden icebox. A small table and one chair. Everything tidy.

Still, my friends and I have put together playhouses better furnished than this.

> I looked up the fish called "buffalo" in Missouri (different fish are called "buffalo" in various parts of the U.S.). It is, according to Wikipedia, "often mislabeled 'buffalo carp' but is not in fact from that family."
>
> It's described as firm-fleshed with few bones, all easily removed, at one time prevalent in midwestern streams draining into the Missouri and Mississippi Rivers. My memory defines it as "delicious."

My aunt places the casserole she carries into the icebox, the fresh-baked rolls onto the table. Then she takes the fruit salad to the cooler, as well, tells me to lay the cake by the rolls.

"Doesn't Uncle Charlie have money to buy food?" I ask.

Aunt Lois laughs. "He's getting along, you know. Late eighties, early nineties. But still fishes year 'round and shares his catch with all of us. Actually, he hasn't been planting a garden these last couple of years."

"Can he live on just fish and maybe blackberries and persimmons, whatever's in season and grows wild?"

Aunt Lois snorts. *He* thinks so. But these days, all of us neighbors take turns getting real food to him. I do every other Friday."

"Won't he be at the picnic?"

"Absolutely! But it never hurts to have a little extra. He's tall, yes, but skinny as a rope—has been, ever since I've known him—weighs maybe a hundred thirty pounds tops."

We go home to pack up some tablecloths and napkins and flatware. Aunt Lois has made a big potato salad, three berry pies, and is adding two quart jars of bread and butter pickles I helped her can last fall before I had to leave the farm and return home to Omaha. I'm so excited, because this is the first time for me to be on the farm early enough in the summer for the Independence Day Community Fish Feed.

"Did Uncle Charlie ever have other family, do you think?" I'm now sharing the back seat of the Pontiac with our picnic supplies. Uncle Jim is driving, Aunt Lois next to him, and we're on our way!

"Not such's anyone around here ever heard about," my aunt says.

Uncle Jim clears his throat. "The man's a mystery, always has been. A local legend."

Then Aunt Lois picks up the story. "Just a kid, a teenager maybe fourteen, fifteen—not that many years older than you are right now."

"After the Civil War, so goes the story," Uncle Jim adds. "Said his folks and family were scattered and gone, so asks could he help out on some farm for food and a place to sleep."

Aunt Lois laughs. "And of course he could. Just room and board? I bet people argued over who got him. Especially when it turned out he did good work—according to the old stories, since no one alive now was an adult here when that young 'Charlie' appeared. Benson's grandfather kept him a long time, then gave him a little chunk of land from Benson's own acreage, right where we were this morning—surveyed it off and signed it legal—so's the boy could have his own place, what Old Man Benson called 'some independence.'"

It's hard for me to imagine Uncle Charlie as a boy. To me, he's always been old but lively. "So he isn't *really* my uncle?" I inquire, disappointed. I've always figured him to be a relative. That other people call him "Uncle Charlie" was beside the point.

"He's everybody's uncle," Aunt Lois assures me.

"But no actual kin to anyone around here," Uncle Jim finishes as he stops the car to open a wire gate on the road leading to bottom land and river property.

I lie back in the comfortable car seat, thinking about Uncle Charlie and about this long-awaited Fourth of July picnic and about what a bright sunny day it is . . . and it's going to be very hot, kind of breathless already, no breeze, sun burning down . . . warm, and I doze.

I am happy enough to play right field—a spot not contested—while sunglare pounds down on all of us. I *love* to play softball. I hope my team members will soon see that I can catch just about anything today because I have my own glove that I brought from home. I hope they'll see that I can also hit far and run fast . . . so then they'll pay no mind to my terrible throwing. Perhaps a high fly will come out here, and no one on base, so that I can take my time getting the ball back.

But nothing at all is happening in right field—that's how it *is* in right field—and my side goes up to bat three times without me getting to the plate because there are so many players on each side. Most are my age or older, but some little ones are in the mix. It's still early in the afternoon. We are all chock full of deep-fried buffalo and the yummy wonders of a rural potluck. Dessert will be later.

So still and quiet. . . . I have time to notice birds flying overhead. Watch action on the infield. Even pay attention to weather. The wind was blowing when we came up here, but now no leaf stirs any of the trees surrounding our playing field.

Sun. Nothing happening, not here on the ballfield nor in the air.

Uncle Jim and Mr. Benson come up through the timber from the picnic area lugging a tub of ice water between them, half a dozen tin ladles jangling over the side.

"Boyd Allen, you stop pitching for a spell," Mr. Benson calls to his son. He wants to interrupt the game because it's so hot and he says a storm may be coming.

This is the first break—and welcome to me, anyway—other than going on and off the field during the endless innings. I don't know the game score. I doubt whether anyone does. Or cares.

Everybody has a drink, then goes over behind the big, homemade backstop if his or her side is "up" and out to the ballfield if not. And from out here, when I get back into right field, I notice that the sky has turned kind of yellowish. Still no air moving, but I feel prickly all over. I see that the down on my arms is standing straight up. A shiver tightens my muscles, and I feel cold in spite of the heat. Over one hundred degrees, Uncle Jim reported from the barn thermometer just before we left to come here about noon today. Still plenty hot, but maybe not *so* warm right now.

I look around the field to see if anyone else appears un-easy. Well, no. But right field is a good place for "noticing" stuff because not all that much ever happens there. And besides, I probably don't *look* to be uneasy myself, if anyone were watching, which no one is. But I am kind of jumpy. Like waiting for thunder after I've seen lightning nearby.

Now Uncle Charlie comes striding in from the trees be-yond third base. He must have been watching our game from the shade.

"You young ones git t'cover," he calls out. "She's agonna blow!"

Nothing happens. No one gives any evidence of having heard him. Boyd Allen pitches another ball. The batter puts a hard grounder right into the hands of the main shortstop (we have three).

I draw in breath. I exhale. My body wants to do something—what's this "cover" Uncle Charlie wants us to get to? Who is this "she"? Is someone going to blow bubbles or what?

Uncle Charlie walks right over onto the infield. "Boyd-Allen, y'all jist toss the ball t'me, son."

Boyd-Allen throws the ball over obediently, and Uncle Charlie catches it. "Now you kids *git!*" the old man orders. "Go he'p your moms and daddies gather up the picnic stuff. You tell 'em there's gonna be a bad blow, and that's f'sure!"

Becky Ann Benson's on first base. "Come on, Uncle Charlie. Look at that bright sun!"

"Uh-huh, an' look't them ornery yellow-black clouds dancin' in fast from the southwest!"

I look behind me and am startled by ugly thunderheads tumbling together.

Boyd-Allen is eldest of us kids, and biggest, so kind of our boss. He says, "Uncle Charlie, our folks'll come up here, they've a mind to have us stop."

The old man's voice is suddenly strong although no louder than before, every syllable ringing in the still air. "Your folks cain't see the sky from down there in them trees. Y'all need to tell 'em t'take a look!"

Uncle Charlie drops the ball right where he stands between pitcher and shortstop. He walks behind the pitcher's mound where Boyd Allen is still standing, over to the first base line, swerves on past me in right field to the middle of the pasture beyond. There, he stands gazing at the southwestern sky.

"Uncle Charlie!" Boyd-Allen calls, "we'll stop the game, do the clouds begin to move in . . . all right?"

His skinny back to all of us and leaning on his crookedy walking stick, Uncle Charlie doesn't respond.

Little Sarah Maude Benson speaks up from her position as "missed-ball runner" behind the two boys covering third base. "Well, *I* don't think y'all are one bit nice to Uncle Charlie when he's our good friend."

"Pitch up, Boyd-Allen!" yells a tall third baseman, and the game recommences.

Sarah Maude marches across the base line defiantly as a grounder misses her by what looks like a couple of inches. At second base, she makes a beeline for Uncle Charlie. She takes his hand that's not grasping the stick, turns her back to the game and watches the sky with him.

I have to admire little Sarah Maude. Only nine years old, but when she believes something she really takes a stand. And she believes in Uncle Charlie. Well, so do I. Unfortunately, I tend to be the "wait and see" type and I need to change my ways. What is this "blow" the man is threatening? And what is the meaning of those churning clouds up there in an otherwise sunny sky? And the sulphury air—what's *that* about?

Sarah Maude is right, too. Uncle Charlie *is* our friend, and no one *has* paid proper attention. Even if his warning is a false alarm, I should at least have the courtesy . . .

A fly ball to right field! Coming in short to me! Glory be! Take your time, girl. Don't overrun it! Go, go, ah-hh! I feel the globe strike my mitt and nestle there. Batter's out. Now what about—get it to second? I pull my arm back, turn slightly to put my weight behind it, throw—eh-hh! *Plop, roll, stop* . . . about two-thirds of the way between me and the second baseman now running back for it. My team members all groan. The runner is headed for third and makes it. I am of course mortified.

"Jiminy! You shoulda throwed it t'third!" yells one of the shortstops.

"Yeah, well, she's only a girl!" laughs a third baseman.

"A *city* girl!" adds the shortstop.

I stand silent in total chagrin.

"So what's wrong with *that!?*" Becky Ann Foley bristles from where she stands to be next batter up and adds, *"Some* girls can throw!" Becky Ann can, I've noticed.

"Yeah, but not when they're from the city, *too,*" somebody on the team-at-bat voices from behind the batter's fence.

Misery, that's me. *Please, God, give me a chance to bat and run the bases.* I hear but barely heed the argument among players regarding girls' playing ball. *City* girls especially. And I am thankful each time the ball is hit that it doesn't come to right field from which I'd have to throw again. But nosirree, I won't get mad and quit. They'll have to ask me not to play, and Aunt Lois's students won't ask their school teacher's niece to leave the field. Ha!

I stifle a giggle. They have a dilemma, don't they? *Come on! Let me bat and run! I don't think anyone even noticed how well I caught the ball.*

One more inning come and gone, and I've still not made it to the batter's box. At least twenty kids are on each team. Back on my bit of right field turf, I feel a whisper of breeze brush my face. I glance back at Uncle Charlie. Sarah Maude is still out there with him. The two are huddled together, and Uncle Charlie has his knobby walking stick pointed at the angry sky and shaking.

In another moment, the whisper has become a breeze. Other team members are noticing the change, as well, looking over at each other, glancing quickly up at the clouds, kind of uneasy like me.

Now a wind. Cool, actually, but too humid to be refreshing. I look up to inspect the southwest where shadowy clouds swarm forward, the darkest filled with flash. Some of those thunderheads have become great black fists filled with lightning. Some have accusing fingers pointed down toward the ground.

I hear a roar building . . . and now a continuing bellow that sounds like the engine of a monster train, overloaded but grinding steadily up a really steep mountain.

My eyes drop to Uncle Charlie and Sarah Maude Benson. The old man is peeling the little girl's hand away from his own, pushing her back into the playing field, shouting to me. "Get her! Get down! Twister for sure!"

And mostly because I don't know what else to do as I lean into the gale to stay upright—and haven't a clue about what a "twister" might be—I hold out my arms to Sarah Maude, who is running before the wind. I grasp and cling to her when she comes to me pellmell.

Now Boyd Allen Benson grabs my shoulder, roughly turns me, hurls me to the ground, taking Sarah Maude with me. He kneels beside us, his arm pinning us, his mouth to my ear.

"Stay down!" he repeats over and again. "Feet t'the wind! Don't run, lie flat as fritters! Stay together!"

I look over at him. Everything in me wants to leap up, grab Sarah Maude's hand and run away from the wind and the sound. But something solid is in Boyd Allen's eyes, a strong set to his face. I'll do what he says.

"Gotta find my other sisters!" he yells as he gets up and moves away. "Pray t'God!" And he's gone.

I see him lurch before the wind toward a group huddled beyond and downwind of the now-billowing wire enclosure which marks the batting area. My arm clutching Sarah Maude close, I twist my head so that I see although not hear Boyd Allen shout at the players, see some of them crawl around the edge of the wire to the upwind side, see him drag three more ballplayers around to there, one by one. It's then that I notice the heavy upright posts holding the wire . . . bending, and one crashes down as I watch, bringing with it a section of cage wire onto the place where the kids had been. Another falls. I can't see Boyd Allen anymore. He's probably lying with the others, upwind of the wire. Inexplicably, I consider whether he's had time to point his feet into the wind.

I turn my head back, the gale snatching at my eyelids and rushing up my nostrils. Uncle Charlie still stands in the pasture, bald head and spindling arms raised to the clouds, his walking stick in hand and churning. He is angled strangely into the blast, a canted silhouette against a fulvous sky.

I open my mouth to call out to him, to tell him to lie down—yes, yes! Put his feet to the wind. But the storm races into my mouth and I hear no words.

The roar is now beyond anything I could have imagined, a pandemonium engulfing us in a great maw of cacophony, somehow striking and numbing each of my other senses. My mouth is dry. My vision is blurred. I feel no pressure from the ground, only my arm tight around Sarah Maude, her small body tucked against mine. But in my head is certainty that danger is whirling onto our pasture.

In fact, though, I feel calm. I am engulfed by the turbulence. So we are safe? I look around at the playing field. Dark patches in the lespedeza ground cover press to the earth and frame shadowy mounds about the area which was our ballfield fewer than five minutes ago. These are other players, I know. Lying flat. I wonder if their feet are to the wind so as to slice the power.

And I'm worried about Aunt Lois and Uncle Jim down there in the trees with the giant blast breaking and tossing at least the topmost branches, what we can see. They'll be worried about me, too. They can't know that Sarah Maude and I are just fine up here, protected by sound . . . clamor . . . roaring racket . . . this incredible noise.

Again I turn back to see Uncle Charlie just as a colossal black funnel comes in from over the far trees above the river and the picnic tables. I wonder if it has blown out the fires beneath the cooking cauldrons or if it has even actually reached the ground so far below. Until now, that is. Because up here, a whirling finger is descending.

I fasten my eyes on Uncle Charlie, watch him standing there, legs apart, the knobby old walking stick raised and shaking into the wind.

I see darkness engulf him as the tube touches down.

And I see the black funnel move away from us and the others, turn across to trees on the far side of the clearing, then bound up above the timberline.

I watch the roiling shadow gradually disintegrate and blend with other darknesses in the sky, see new black shapes in the near distance, smaller ones emerge and recede, bounce down, hover, leave.

And then it's over. The roar is diminishing and now gone. The wind is coming still, but in gusts—warmer, less violent. And the rain begins, heavy drops bolstered by white pellets of hail bouncing on the earth all around us, pounding my bare neck, my arms and legs. Then I remember the little girl beside me.

I pull Sarah Maude even closer as I realize that she's wracked with sobs. "It's all right," I tell her. "The storm's going away, Honey. . . . You're going to be fine."

"Uncle Charlie!" the child gasps. "Where's Uncle Charlie?"

I look back. A few minutes ago, I was fascinated by the hovering cloud, horrified but also mesmerized by its approach, then relieved by its departure. I saw it come down to and envelop the old man, then turn away from the playing field. I followed its progress to the trees, gaped at its metamorphosis in the upper air, admired the miniatures which followed it and dissipated. . . . *But now where is Uncle Charlie?*

My Uncle Jim walks into the back lean-to well after supper time on the Tuesday evening following the picnic. "They've called off the search." He removes his straw hat, places it carefully on the high peg over the bench. I see that his eyelids droop. He does not agree with the decision, I can tell.

"Oh, Jim!" That's Aunt Lois.

"But—" I object, then find no words to finish.

"You know that he couldn't still be alive." Aunt Lois tries to comfort him. She puts an arm across his shoulders. "You know he's not somewhere suffering."

"Do I?" Uncle Jim asks.

I am relieved by my aunt's words. My imagination has had Uncle Charlie hanging up helpless in a tree somewhere, ever since last Friday, thirsty and slowly starving to death. But what do I know about tornados? Nothing? Not much. I hurry into the kitchen to put my uncle's food back on the range for warming. My tears drop and sizzle on the black iron. My papa died several years ago. But first he got sick. Then he went to the hospital. Then he died. There was a funeral, and I know absolutely where he is buried.

But with Uncle Charlie, he was here one moment, then gone in the next. And now it looks as if he'll never return.

At the table, my uncle directs his fork to his mouth, for once not much interested in food. "Strange thing about tornados," he tells my aunt and me. "They sometimes seem to mix up the molecules. Make illogical things happen."

Aunt Lois nods. "Like that long broom straw stuck clean through the thick trunk of Mother's big maple tree, back home in Kansas."

"Exactly." Uncle Jim is chewing.

"And a whole house picked up and deposited gollywampus facing another direction, but not a dish broken, nothing and no one damaged."

"Those are the rare, lucky ones," Uncle Jim agrees, pushing back from the table while I think about Dorothy and the Wizard of Oz.

"Well, he left us as he came—just 'appeared' maybe seventy years ago. An adolescent. People thought his parents or relatives would come looking, so the story goes. But no one ever showed up." Aunt Lois sighs. "And now he's gone without a trace—disappeared right out into the ether."

My aunt tends to notice the jokes that life plays on people. She calls them "irony." Strange term, I think then and still do.

Someone picked up Uncle Charlie's gnarled walking stick from where he stood in the field of lespedeza that day, looking into the storm. But that was it. Uncle Charlie disappeared, definitely, and then was gone forever without a trace. Aunt Lois is right about the irony of his life. He arrived here in the Missouri hills alone out of no one knew where, all those years back. And then he left this place.

I remember how fiercely he faced the twister on that day, as if to single-handedly save all of us children up there on the ballfield—just he and that walking stick. And who knows? Perhaps he *did* save us on that day.

And I consider how he lived so long, most of his life right here as part of this community, respected and cared for by everyone and especially loved by the children. But still always alone, never part of any particular family. An independent man who lived independently and then vanished on Independence Day.

6

(Preferences)

Over or Under?

Heloise, bless her dear domestic soul, made a mistake when she dodged a question by a reader of her popular home advice column. The inquiry: "Is bathroom tissue properly dispensed from *under* or *over* the roller?" Heloise's response, in effect: "Who cares?"

Although the matter was never resolved, it turned out that a great many people *cared.* She received hundreds of cards and letters from all over the world, and each writer had a strong and certain opinion—and presented her (and sometimes *his*) own version of logical substantiation. Those touting *under* repeatedly cited sanitation and economy. Those recommending *over* talked of accessibility and generosity. Both sides of the dialogue insisted that the roll is *wrapped* to be dispensed under (or over), that it is easier to unroll when coming out over (or under), that it is visually more appealing when the tissue comes out under (or over), that any design on the paper can be in place only when the roll comes out over (or under) and—most of all—it is by-heaven *correct* to bring the paper out under (or over) the roll.

As mail continued not for weeks but for months, no preponderance of responses emerged to weigh heavily either way.

Thus, the beleaguered but nevertheless amused Heloise could not report a "majority" on either side. No democratic vote was going to allow closure on this mighty matter. As the issue was gradually replaced by more timely concerns, one impression remained. . . . Many people *do* care about which way the paper rolls.

And you know what? *I care,* too! Any bathroom tissue over which I have control will by-God come out *over the top*—not because this is necessarily "correct" or because the paper is wrapped that way or because appearance is thereby improved (although I'm willing to debate this latter).

Some subjects domestic are important; others not. For instance, although I *know* that the fold of the napkin at table goes against the diner's tummy, I don't know why and would hesitate to hypothesize. My eighth grade teacher taught us students that particular convention—and *no one* second-guesses an Eighth Grade Teacher. Also, my fussy Aunt Myrtle convinced me some three-score years ago that my family's health and perhaps the health of future generations depended directly on my placing freshly-dried tumblers with the opening *up* (not down) on the pantry shelf—something about not providing a still-moist nursery for bacteria growth—a practice I observe to this day.

And then there are of course such not-so-important household subjects—the *real* "Who cares?" of daily living. Most people would concede the unimportance of which finger flips a light switch, which foot steps first into a shoe, what laundry load order should be . . . you get the idea. But on this matter of bathroom tissue, let me explain.

I grew up in the Depression, and it was my mother's thrift, I realize now, that got us so handily through those cash-poor days. Still, certain among her pronouncements were difficult to abide by, and I remember the toilet tissue issue with particular clarity. First, the paper was to wind out from *under* the roll—absolutely!—and was to consist of no more than four sheets, one person's share. Coming from *under,* according to Mother, made the paper harder to access and easier to control as to amount. Ok.

Some teenagers rebel by misrepresenting where they are going or with whom to do what. Not I. My crime took a different course: I used *six* and one time *seven* sheets off the roll during a single restroom visit. And because I was brought up not only in the Depression but also in a pious Baptist household, I still six decades later suffer guilt pangs from that thievery.

Somewhere around age ten, probably an early symptom of rebellion, I vowed that when I had a home of my own, the bathroom tissue would always come out *over* the roll—accessible! And that pledge I have kept, even when the going got rough.

My family and I lived for several years on the island of Ponape (now *Pohnpei)* in the Central Pacific. Everything that got to us from "abroad" had spent a minimum of two years in the hold of a ship cruising the tropics. Toilet tissue was not—in the opinion of whoever made decisions on stocking a supply ship—worthy of export/import. Probably, too much bulk for the price it could command. Bottom line (so to speak), my children and I spent Sunday afternoons on my Honda 90 trail bike searching for said tissue.

We three traversed foot paths up into the rainforest, trails which led to tiny village stores that might—just *might* have a roll or two or even three available. The stuff was always the same brand, something brought to the island in cases by fishing boats from Fiji, each roll about two inches in diameter and having texture and color suggesting de-hydrogenated bay reeds, so practically guaranteed to give slivers. But the rolls were reasonably priced and—mercifully—*available* to those willing to shop the boonies.

I'm telling this to make my point: even *then,* during a time when bathroom tissue was the prize result of serious scavenging, the paper in a bathroom at my house came out from the dispenser *over* the roll.

As it does today. Come visit. Feel free to use the restroom if you need to rest. And take all the sheets you fancy, no one's counting. In fact, I'm from the Midwest; and as my guest, you are my concern. I *care.* So go ahead, if you like: take the whole darned roll!

7

No White Elephants, Please

"Throw it *away?*" My voice probably vibrated with outrage and disappointment. "But it's worth a lot to me—I've had it *forever!*" At least that long—and possibly in a former life besides! How could my husband be so insensitive?

If you're a collector, then you know how the next exchanges went: "At least let me *give* it to someone" and "Who'd want it?" and "My great-great grandmother may have brought that from England with her when she eloped with her coachman" and "It says 'Made in China' on the bottom." (I hadn't expected to win that one. I bought the jelly dish for 10¢ at a schoolyard rummage sale when I was in third grade. But I'm seventy-one now; that dish and I are *old*.)

Long sigh from my non-collecting husband: "Another white elephant."

These days, a *white elephant* refers to something which may be beautiful and even valuable—but is of no use to its owner. It's that statue or wooden box or bone-dish which sits around taking up space and demanding that you dust it. But where does the term come from?

In India and much of Southeast Asia, elephants are still used for heavy work (mostly logging) and for human transportation. And white elephants there are both *real* and *rare*. They are albino (or part albino). And a fully (or even "largely") albino elephant put to work would not be likely to survive the sun in those countries where elephants live.

A white elephant is usually beautiful, but it often means trouble for its owner. Here is this big creature that eats and drinks as much as any other elephant (lots!) but cannot be nearly so useful. Why not?

What is Albino?

An *albino* is any living creature, human or other animal—which has a marked lack of coloring (pigmentation) for skin and hair. So the *albino* is a very pale version of others among its same species. *Albinism* is present at birth or hatching.

The condition is the result of doubling a certain recessive gene. That is, both "parents" must contribute a gene or no degree of *albinism* is possible.

An albino person is extremely pale with white or near-white hair and can have pink eyes (capillaries), even if the person is born into a family having African-American or Hispanic or other olive-complexioned and brown-eyed origins.

Albino people and animals have to stay out of the sun because it is this pigmentation (which they lack) that protects them from the sun's rays. Their eyes are particularly sensitive to light and easily injured.

The countries where varieties of the Asian elephant occur—including such places as India and Malaysia, Nepal and

Sri Lanka—are drenched with sunlight on most days of most seasons every year. Like people, elephants tend to be diurnal. Work and travel by elephant happen in the daytime. But the white elephant can be permanently blinded by too-bright light. Its skin can be fatally burned by sustained sunshine. So unless the activity happens to take place in dense forest shade or at night, an albino elephant cannot be used.

Also, the albino of any species is delicate, requiring extra care and concern for health. So here is the owner, responsible for the feeding and fitness of this huge creature—a monster eating machine which all too easily becomes ill. A fully grown pachyderm can consume daily four hundred pounds of food and more than forty gallons of water. But the owner gets little or no payback for the trouble and expense. He could try to sell the attractive animal. But who wants a white elephant? Who would want to take on all that work and worry for a handsome but essentially useless beast?

For centuries, people in Thailand were exceptionally sad to find themselves in possession of a white elephant. Beside the normal problems, albinos by law became automatically "owned" by the king. Regardless of location in the country, and from the moment of birth, a white elephant automatically belonged to the monarch. After it could leave its mother, it usually went to live a pampered but idle life on palace grounds. The former owner might have the responsibility for keeping the creature healthy and might have to feed it lots of vegetation every day—and in fact was often *required* to do so. But no one was allowed to work or ride a white elephant. All were the prized and sacred property of the king.

How does someone *get* a white elephant? A gravid wild elephant captured and tamed might give birth to an albino (or near-albino) baby. Or one might be born to domestic stock on a farm or camp where elephants are kept. But in Thailand, someone could suddenly get a white elephant in still another way. Or at least get the full care and responsibility for one. The king could "give" it to you.

When a prominent politician or public leader annoyed the king, the regent would get even. With great ceremony and many smiles, the monarch would present his enemy with this very special gift: a white elephant. A peculiar possession. The person receiving the present had full responsibility for food and health, but the creature remained forever under royal protection. The new "owner" couldn't even take a ride on it in the safety of a dark night. Imagine what a drain on purse and energy this kind of ownership meant to someone living in a city. And if the person continued to irritate the monarch, his royal highness was not above giving two or three *more* white elephant "awards" to the troublemaker. . . .

All of passing interest, you say? But meantime, I have on my shelves and in cabinets at home these dozens and dozens of *white elephants*. . . .

That Compelling Voice

Lucy from *Peanuts* talks a lot. She'd be an author if she could write. Mostly, she's full of herself: often mistaken but never in doubt. She speaks loudly and with great conviction. In fact, Lucy's so sure of herself that she tells us the only error she's ever made happened once when she *thought* she was wrong but wasn't.

A disgruntled Charlie Brown observes repeatedly, "Lucy's not always right—she just **sounds** right!"

We as writers need to copy a leaf from Lucy's binder. We need not only to *be* right but also to *sound* right. We must walk with solid steps along the corridors where readers dwell. Not pussyfoot.

When and where do we learn all this humility? Society is one villain. Modest Mode is cultivated more often and to greater depth among females of our species—but less often now than in the past. I wanted to initiate that last phrase with "perhaps" or even a daring "probably," then stopped myself. . . .

Men, however, are not excluded from the Malady of

Meekness. And more frequently than women, males fall victim to Society's partner in crime: the *Objective Viewpoint* as dictated by science. In addition to branding as *uncool* any passion and enthusiasm in writing—signaling lack of discipline if nothing nastier—we are taught early on to avoid comprehensive statements unless true in all instances. Depending on how deeply scientific tenets are ingrained, we qualify, qualify, qualify . . . *such and such is likely to be true in most cases when particular circumstances prevail and if the requisite conditions are present in sufficient form and quantity.*

And with these qualifiers and restraints we manage to distance ourselves from responsibility and our reader from everything we write. Oh yeah, I confess. I am a woman born in the 'Thirties with an undergraduate major in Science. Can there be any hope at all for someone so encumbered?

A soft voice might be soothing but it's mighty hard to hear. Compare some couplings which follow. I didn't choose unforgettable passages from Timeless Literature. Rather, I plucked up narrative segments that illustrate the compelling voice of several distinguished writers.

1a. Lee Chong's grocery story was often littered and somewhat messy, but it frequently offered a wide variety of merchandise to the persevering and determined customer.

Like it? Try discarding the six qualifiers. Now compare what's above to this opening from Steinbeck's *Cannery Row.* More than brevity is at work.

1b. Lee Chong's grocery, while not a model of neatness, was a miracle of supply.

Try these two which follow, and decide which was written by E. Annie Proulx in *Shipping News*:

2a. **Quoyle gasped, the phone to his ear, loss flooding in like the sea into a broken hull.**

2b. **Quoyle fairly wheezed into the mouthpiece, as if the wildly unwelcome news about the probable loss of his wife took most of his breath, a vastly unexpected strong blow to the belly.**

Decide which of the next two lines speaks with the stronger voice. You were correct in choosing 2a from the pair above.

3a. **He apologized to her for the condition of the country, with the result that she gave one of her sudden little shoots of tears.**

3b. **When he tried to apologize abjectly to her for the dilapidated surroundings, she became somewhat sad and gradually started to cry.**

One of the above is from E.M. Forster's *Passage to India*. Can there be any doubt as to which selection is in the master's voice?

So. Are we now determined to squelch the qualifiers in our work? To march firmly forward in full confidence? To express ourselves with certainty? To *stop waffling?!?*

Charles Dickens created a sticky fellow named Uriah Heep. Bigger than life, this minor clerk made a religion of fawning. Throughout most of the book, Heep was a model of meek, the prototype of paltry—such a spineless lump of lowliness as to make one's skin crawl. When you find yourself sinking into Servile Mode, a good browse of old Uriah in *David Copperfield* may help.

Works for me, anyway. But then, I do have a Heep of humility to unload. . . .

9

Reading The Writing
(An Opinion)

The scene is a college workshop for educated adults interested in writing prose fiction, memoir, genealogy, and commercial articles or even books. The subject varies according to focus and style for each participant. The procedure is to read portions of one's work aloud and pick through listener's comments, whether spoken or written, with the object of improving the material.

But the *reading*—ah! Those immortal phrases set on paper . . . do we fling them dramatically into the ether? Do we murmur them humbly in hope that a listener who cannot understand the words will not be too disparaging in the critique? Let us digress with relevance . . .

Dr. Ralph Wardle, one time head of the English Department at the University of Nebraska, was the best teacher I ever had. Small, sandy, dapper—always beige suited, vested and conservatively necktied, I can still see him perched on the forward right corner of the desk in whatever room he had been assigned, one haunch and knee crooked on the ledge, the other down and bracing. The professor had a broad and penetrating knowledge, quirky humor, well-merited confidence—and fixed notions on all matters within his domain. He told us once (as I recall) that George Orwell was a perpetually unhappy man who ended his own life by walking into the sea. I have since read some quite different accounts of his demise. Those biographies simply got it wrong—I will believe forever what Dr. Wardle said. My professor probably had his shoes off and pant legs rolled up to watch it all happen from shore.

A stern taskmaster with high standards, Dr. W. didn't just *sound* right—he *was* right about everything on which he reported or expressed opinion. Or so I believed then and still do. Thus, I shall defer to his practices in the writing seminars he conducted. In a sense, to do this is to cheat. You can argue with me—your opinion is as good as mine. But no one *anywhere* can challenge that great professor, may he rest in peace.

"When you read your work aloud for the group, you simply read the words you have written with fair speed, enunciating clearly and imparting no particular emphasis," said he. **"That way, what you have written—those particular words in that specific order—are the bases for assessment. The quality of your delivery is alien to your document, a dimension with which we must not be concerned. Printed matter is, after all, *only* that. Success and failure are based on the ideas and images which *your words on the printed page* convey *to* and invoke *in* the reader."**

Dr. Wardle laid out criteria for our reading and then enforced these standards. Observed in his seminar and subsequently, I have recognized six types of readers evident in any kind of workshop where a writer reads aloud for critique by other members of the group—and this whether or not the listener has a copy of the work to read along (and mark). The categories were evident a thousand years ago when I was doing undergraduate work and are evident also in a 21st Century assembly of reasonably mature people experienced with life. How would the professor respond to these types?

First, we have the *Stumbler*. This shy type gets stagestruck when required to read aloud. Never mind the labor of many hours over every paragraph, sentence, phrase, verily every word and syllable in this manuscript. The tongue thickens, breath is labored, eyes blur, birdflesh rises on the forearms. *My God, who flung this mish-mash onto the page? Did this come here by alien saboteurs? I have never before seen these words in this order. What idiot penned such crap?* The reader puffs along, stopping for breath, mispronouncing words, omitting others, re-reading frequently, perspiring and choking until the merciful end.

Actually, in Dr. Wardle's group, the end is a point some few sentences after the beginning when the manuscript is removed from the sufferer and handed over to a neighbor in the classroom.

"From the beginning, if you please."

"Any author is free," the professor intones without passion, "and is in fact encouraged to ask another member of the group to read if an oral reading problem exists."

A *stumbler* who dares to attempt a repeat performance loses his or her document to Dr. Wardle's firm fingers and next sees it only as a red-penciled essay graded and returned without benefit of audition.

The second type of reader is the *Mumbler*. This one is reading steadily, most likely, for he or she turns pages regularly.

No one in the group knows what is on those pages, however, because the Mumbler is—apparently—reading to him- or herself for personal pleasure.

"Speak up!" Dr. Wardle will command. And if the reader does not do so immediately, the manuscript is removed from the writer and once again handed to another group member for reading.

Again: "From the beginning."

The third type of reader is the *Orator*. This serious person, like Demosthenes, has been walking around with rocks in the mouth all week in order to make what is written *Per-fect-ly Clear*. This one eyes the audience and then begins. Ponderously. Each word, each syllable is emphasized. This is Wise Stuff. Nod. This is Funny Stuff. Chuckle. This is Sad Stuff. Weep.

In the silence following conclusion, the reader looks to the group with satisfaction. The listeners are stunned—as they *should* be. Actually, the material really *might have been* canny . . . clever . . . or/and filled with pathos. Possibly all three and more. But the silence of the group has to do with separating the words from their declamation. With trying to recall the meaning of the material rather than the manner of its presentation.

This reader must surely puzzle the professor. Certainly the group has heard and understood ev . . . er . . . y . . . sin . . . gle . . . syl . . . la . . . ble. But how does someone assess the words written when delivery is so ponderous? The professor in this instance will "wind forward" from the wrist with his right hand during the reading and frown mildly afterward . . . but let the matter pass.

The fourth type of reader is the *Speed Demon*. The words are read with sufficient volume and clear enunciation, yes—but at NASCAR tempo. Does the reader believe that his or her writing is not worthy of class time? Is the reader fearful of interruption? Power outtage? Earthquake? Personal demise? Is the manuscript too long, so that the reader hopes reading at triple speed will allow him or her to dash through the entirety in a third the time?

Dr. Wardle's solution for this reader is a growled, "Slow down!" Simple. Don't argue. Do it!

The fifth reading type is the *Thespian*. He or she reads the work as if performing on stage for a paying audience. The voice rises and falls dramatically, giving way to meaningful pauses. The words of a shouting character are shouted. Those of someone screaming are screamed. Real tears roll off the jaw of the reader when a character is undergoing trauma. Listeners in the group know that they are presented here with a by-God *method actor*. In fact, the workshop participants are so engrossed in the kaleidoscope of emotions—their range! their intensity!—that they have no idea either at the time or later as to whether the ideas promulgated or the words selected to present those ideas have any validity. They DO know that this talented person could read a grocery list with similar insight and depth of feeling.

Dr. Wardle's response to the *Thespian* seems to do the job: "A bit more of the writing, if you please, and a great deal less of *you.*" Ouch.

All of which brings us to the sixth and final type of reader—the reader who presumably has survived previously a writing workshop under Dr. Wardle. This one just "reads." Clear, moderate volume, well enunciated but with no particular inflection. Words float out there to listeners, syllables neither enhanced nor impeded, available for appraisal. For this one—and *only* this one—the good professor nods and smiles.

Do you recognize the reader types? Do you recognize yourself? I found *me*—and unfortunately, I'm not Number Six. Which are you?

10

(The New Genre)

Narrative Nonfiction

So does "Narrative Nonfiction" (NN) provide a fresh and fancy name for Memoir? Brief answer: No. Then is this what some call "Creative Nonfiction"? Yes—but in my opinion wrongly so. Creative Nonfiction sounds to me like an oxymoron, a contradiction of terms: imaginative truth, spoken music. Many fine books of memoir (and autobiography) have been written. NN (and "Creative" Nonfiction) usually refers to shorter works—previously known as essays and/or articles. So let's compare the differences between *short* memoir/autobiography and narrative nonfiction. You will see that the main contrast lies in *focus.*

Memoir is the "true story" of a portion of someone's life. Emphasis tends to be on the author. Narrative nonfiction is a "true story" of one or several related occurrences in an author's life. But emphasis is on the actual "happenings," including the people involved, and only incidentally on the author. Sometimes the NN is in first person, true; but in that case the author tends not to take him/herself too seriously. Memoir and NN start out from different bases, then, different viewpoints on the part of the author. And thus we are talking about "focus."

The writer of memoir believes that events in his or her life have been sufficiently exciting/unique to be of interest to others. Sometimes, this is true. Other times, not so much. Everyone seems to think, in these days of Blog and Twitter and Print on Demand, that he or she can and should even "write a book." And most often, the book in mind is a really long memoir, autobiographical. And hell yes, my life has been *really* interesting to me, so should be to others, and here we go!

Often, the memoir is written in first person, and nothing is intrinsically wrong with that. What gets memoir a bad name is that the writer thinks that every breath taken in the life being recounted is of intense interest to All. Not so. Remember the time Mom organized this humongous birthday party for me and then put the wrong number of candles on the cake? How could the whole world *not* be interested in such an event? You get the idea.

Narrative nonfiction (NN) may be written in first *or* third person. But even in first person, the number of first-person-singular "I"s and "me"s is a fraction of those found in memoir. Narrative nonfiction focuses on action in an event or series of related events. It deals with characterization which naturally involves the author but tends to "point" elsewhere. Simply, the author of narrative nonfiction does *not* take that first person (himself or herself) as the Main Event. When focus in short written work shifts from event/setting/other characters to the author, the work shifts from NN to Memoir.

Here are a couple of first-person samples to help point up these differences:

1. My mother believed that my physical well-being was *my* responsibility, almost regardless of age. Well before I enrolled in kindergarten, I remember being

sent to bed without dinner because I had stepped into the road in front of our house to retrieve a ball—and been knocked over by a bicycle rider. A hard lesson I never forgot!

2.   The bike rider was plummeting down the road at jet speed. And oblivious to surroundings, I was dashing onto the street to retrieve my favorite ball. The bicyclist hit my churning, four-year-old legs a glancing but harmless touch which upended me but sent him reeling into traffic amid blasting horns and angry shouts.

No one was hurt, as it turned out, but many were disturbed and some were angry. Traffic halted to get things sorted out. And of course my Mother happened to be on the front porch to witness the near-disaster. Her face was pale, her eyes were sparking fury, and her arms were akimbo as I ascended the steps, the errant ball tucked firmly under my arm.

She took the ball, tossed it off the end of the porch onto our lawn. "Upstairs!" she commanded. "No dinner, no good-night story. Your day's done."

I plodded up the steps, replaced clothing with jammies, sniffled a bit with a nose running to match tears leaking from my eyes. How could I have done what I did? In our Depression-time household, every person was responsible for keeping his and her own body intact and free from harm. No exceptions. Well, my ball was safe—and from now on would stay in the back yard.

Which of these is the beginning of a narrative nonfiction? And which is memoir? Both are "true," but each is so, so *different*.

11

(Favorites)

Pet Punctuation

Although I think of myself as a writer (as do you, or you wouldn't be reading this), I do when the cupboard is bare put on my line editor cap for a couple of small publishers and the swarm of writers planning to self publish. And over the years, I have noticed that *most* authors have a highly favored mark of punctuation which they tend to overuse. I'm no exception, by the way, but of course *my* pet punctuation is special and always appropriate. But we'll get to that later. . . .

Dominating the field for most frequently cuddled Pet in the Punctuation Kennel is of course the universal and all-encompassing comma. There may be a special place (hopefully uncomfortable) in the afterlife for primary-school teachers (and those of middle and junior and even high school, Lord help us!) who instruct students in their writing to use a comma "whenever there's a pause." Apparently, this is the one lesson *no kid ever forgets.*

From the very beginning, all of us who write are of course producing Deathless Prose to live forever in the hearts of mankind. Therefore, we want our words read (aloud or silently) with appropriate dignity and aplomb—employing lots of pauses so that everyone "gets it."

Commas, then. A multitude of commas. A plethora of them. A veritable infinitude of the damn things. I have to hold myself back, when editing, from twisting off their little tails and capitalizing the next word for a "new sentence." But we all know that's not fair. Commas have their places, right? In fact, a great many places.

Commas

We know the rules. Place a comma (a) before the conjunction in a compound sentence and (b) to separate words in a series (except last two items if they're already separated by "or" or "and"). In dates, (c) separate day from year and (if part of a sentence ongoing), year from the rest of the sentence. Similarly, a comma (d) separates city from state and/or country and (if part of a sentence ongoing) state or country from the remainder of the sentence.

We also use a comma (e) to attach words/phrases to the beginning or end of a sentence. Something like "Yes" or "Certainly" or "By the way," usually at the beginning, occasionally at the end. Also, we use the comma to set off someone's name or title—a term of direct address: "Fred, come here." And finally, appositives get the comma treatment: "Fred, who is my eldest brother, comes into the room." If that "attachment" occurs in the middle of the sentence, we set it off on both sides. Related to the above but slightly different, we use the comma to (f) set off from the rest of the sentence something not essential to the meaning, but nevertheless relaying additional information. (See em dash later.)

But the overriding rule on commas is to use one to prevent reader misunderstanding. If there's no chance of that, never mind the rule (or the comma). For example, in "He told a joke and I laughed," it would be silly to stick a comma before that conjunction "and."

Semicolons

Among us are those writers who adopt semicolons as their punctuation of choice.

I think of semi colons as "SUPER commas." A semi colon within a compound sentence means that one does not need to have a conjunction. But put <u>only</u> a comma between clauses in a compound sentence and you have yourself the *dreaded comma splice!* (Put two clauses together without benefit of comma/conjunction OR semi colon, and you have committed a *run-on sentence,* and all hope is lost.)

"Super" status for the semi colon comes when it's used to prevent confusion by separating major groups in a series from minor groups in the same series, as follows:

"She has lived for two or more years of her life in Sedalia, Missouri; Rome, Italy; Peterborough, New Hampshire; Pagan, Mariana Islands; and Chico, California."

You can see that deciphering the above would be a mess without the "super comma" semi colons.

Colons

Although few writers whose manuscripts I read "domesticate" colons and overuse them, even fewer restrict them to "proper" use. A colon is a pointer. You can substitute for it the word(s) "thus" or "namely" or "as follows." That colon tells the reader, "Here it is, specifically!"

However (always an exception, right?), we do not EVER use a colon immediately after a verb, and especially not after a verb of being. The verb is already pointing the way, so a colon placed after that verb is redundant.

Traditionally, a couple of spaces follow a colon. These green days, one. Just be consistent.

Hyphens

The friendly little hyphen (single dash on keyboard) is used to join compound words (check dictionary) and *to compound* words. An example of the former would be something like hot-wire (starting an engine without a key) not yet in such common usage that it's become one word like "hotbed" or "hotshot" but not so distant as to be fully separate combinations like "hot toddy" and "hot tub."

Adjectives or adverbs that build on each other are normally compounded (so hyphenated) to show their relationship before the noun or verb (or additional adverb) they modify. Examples: "lavender-tinged mountains" and "often-expensive seasonings."

Note that it is generally held that one does NOT compound (hyphenate) with an "-ly" adverb, so should be "barely noticed publication" and NOT "barely-noticed publication." I just recently learned this rule, and I don't like it. But so far, no one in charge of making rules has consulted me.

Dashes

A dash indicates a break in thought. Period. Someone can get very technical about dashes, reaching back to involve the hyphen and then proceeding to the *en* dash and finally the *em* dash. For most purposes (and keyboarders and all but highly scientific writers), the *em dash—three unspaced hyphens*—does the job. This em dash uses the three hyphens without spaces between them and without space after or before text on either side: "My grandmother made sweet rind pickles—my favorites!—from otherwise-useless watermelon rind." You did catch, did you not, my subtle insertion of a compounded modifier?

Few people in my experience have a problem with using dashes. Many people, however, seem to have trouble with controlling them. These writers tend to get carried away by the sheer freedom these marks evoke. Three unspaced hyphens (on my keyboard, anyway) get you a healthy em dash and a comfortable "thought leap" in your manuscript.

However, four or more unspaced hyphens (a really *long* dash) does not increase the drama of such a break. No one I've met (over the age of five) doubles- or triples-up on commas. Or on semi colons. So why do we writers think that a row of fourteen (or thirty-seven) dashes will increase the excitement? To my best knowledge, the only emotion evoked is impatience (by readers) and irritation (by line editors).

Parentheses and Brackets

A long-time friend and English teacher was explaining parentheses to a successful travel writer who lacked formal training.

"See, you put the 'paren' here at the front of your explanatory or additional information, then close it off with a 'thesis' at the end."

Say *what???*

No, no. Just as a colon requires vertical double dots (:) and semi colons require one dot over a comma (;), the parenthesis consists of a pair of marks ( ) which enclose something not necessary to the sentence itself—a bit of extra information, a minor example or two, possibly a brief explanation or author comment.

And then if you want to be brave and increase the complexity, "parenthetical matter" *within* parenthetical matter is enclosed by brackets ([ ]).

Example: **My favorite punctuation (rightly or wrongly [despite prior instruction by well-meaning English teachers] and forever) is the ellipsis.**

Logically, should you wish to further complicate your writing by still another imbedding, you go back to parentheses—and so forth, alternating them. But please! Consider what you're doing to your reader and *don't go there.*

And yes, a space always occurs between outside text and the parenthesis and bracket marks.

Note: brackets are often used independently (not within parentheses) to show *in quoted scientific/mathematic material* what a parenthesis usually shows: extra information, an example, quick explanation, or editor comment.

Quotation Marks (Double And Single)

Most people don't pick quotation marks for favored punctuation, as they're fairly straightforward. American usage begins with the double quotation mark (") to begin a direct quotation *and* to end it ("), with the mark placed after any other punctuation: "I'm going home." A quotation within a quotation moves to the single quotation mark (Fred asked, "Who said, 'I'm going home'?")

British usage differs. There, a direct quotation begins with a single quotation mark: 'I'm going home'. Note that punctuation which follows and relates to entire sentence is *outside* the quotation mark. And thus quite logically, a quotation within a quotation moves to the double quotation mark (Fred asked, 'Who said, "I'm going home"?'

The Lovely Ellipsis

And here is my own personal downfall. The ellipsis consists of three spaced dots: . . . (*un*spaced if you're going green)—and not five or twenty! More than three (with one exception) are merely "a bunch of dots." The exception occurs when the ellipsis is placed at the end of a completed declarative sentence. . . . As done in the immediately foregoing.

All right, I admit it. Ellipses can be overused—and I'm guilty! Used with discretion, though (something I work hard to achieve) ellipses can be a means to ensure partnership between writer and reader.

So let's take a look first at some ways that ellipses can be used legitimately:

a. First, we frequently employ an ellipsis to flag the intentional omission of words. Thus, we avoid specifying to the acrid end something fully predictable and wordy. Here are several examples:

1. My three-year-old started counting with "one" and moved along until he reached his goal: "One, two, three . . . thirty-seven, thirty-eight . . . ninety-nine, a hundred!"

2. The witch placed into her caldron of water an eye of newt, a tail of rat, and the fleshy comb of rooster, then lit the fire. . . .

3. The headless horseman clutched the reins, then dug his heels into the flanks of his steed. . . .

b. Second, the ellipsis can be used to allow each reader to complete an author's premise to the satisfaction of the reader. An example:

"Given three wishes by a bottle genie, my first wish would be . . ."

c. Third, an ellipsis can signal a "thinking" pause in speech: "I think I just got . . . a *job?*"

d. Fourth and finally, the ellipsis can cue either an unfinished thought or a sentence that trails off into silence: "If only I could remember his exact words . . ."

I once had a line editor who "cleansed" every ellipsis from my 250-page manuscript. However, he himself apparently suffered from something I think of as "hyphenitis" (not to be confused with the deadly "comma-itis") so that many compound words *be-came care-fully* hyphened.

Fortunately in this case, the author gets the final word on the pre-print line edit. I will confess here, however, that I replaced only about half of my ellipses. The other half truly were unnecessary. Okay, I'm *working* on it!

12

Finding Something to Say

I never thought I'd live so much of my adult life overseas. That I'd actually get to see exotic places and animals described in books. Unlike many teenagers and young-marrieds, I didn't yearn to travel. Oh, I fantasized about strange-sounding, far-away places: *Kuala Lumpur. Kathmandu.* Soft syllables sweet on the tongue. But to leave the Midwest and home? Probably not.

I was born and grew up in Nebraska, the only child in an extended household that included a schoolmarm Mom, a Baptist pastor Papa, and my maternal Grandmother Larkin. Assorted relatives for reciprocal visiting lived not only there in Omaha but in choice (to me) rural spots of Kansas and Missouri.

But then one condition and four ostensibly unrelated incidents combined to jar and subsequently tip me off my familiar planet. The condition was that most of my immediate family was gone. Papa had died when I was nine, Grandma Larkin when I was eleven—and now very recently Mother when I was almost thirty. The cousins with whom I'd grown up were scattered. I had a few dear friends, but "close family" now consisted of my husband and me plus our son Kent and daughter Karol.

The four impelling incidents?

98

First, I had several years back attended a summer Writing Workshop under Guest Professor Walter Van Tilburg Clark, author of *The Oxbow Incident* and some other (at the time) well respected work. At Workshop conclusion, each participant had a private conference with Dr. Clark during which (he having read all of our writing to date [in my instance, not much!]) he chatted about our "chances" as writers. His message to me: "Phyl, you write very well indeed. Unfortunately, you have nothing to say." This message did not destroy me but certainly caught my attention . . . and probably planted the seed for what was to come.

Second, and some years later, the venerable Clara Sterling retired from the high school where I'd taught English for seven years. She had been teaching her third generation of local families. A pillar of Thomas Jefferson High School, she'd been there forever. She knew what worked and what didn't at the school and in the community of Council Bluffs (across the bridge from Omaha, in Iowa). However could we continue to operate without her?

But then in the serious part of her retirement party, Clara told us with pride (as I remember) that she had never lived nor *wanted* to live anywhere else, had never traveled (nor wanted to) more than fifty miles from home.

No. I much admired this woman, but to spend one's entire life in one spot on this huge and diversified planet? . . . No!

The **third** incident involved my five-year-old son Kent after he received a "scholarship" to attend Saturday-morning art classes in a special Children in the Arts Program at the Joslyn Memorial Museum in Omaha—the city's *only* artistic distinction (my opinion in retrospect) at that time. Proud mama, I braved snow and ice each week throughout Nebraska's vigorous wintertime to drive him to city center for this so-special honor. . . . only to receive at semester's end a mysterious invitation to attend the culminating drama, *Jack and the Beanstalk,* starring (am I ready for this?) my son Kent Brisby. Whoa!

"So you've been going to Performing Arts instead of Art Class every Saturday?"

"Not *every* Saturday, Mom." Scared. "Was that a bad thing to do?"

"Not *bad,* Honey. It's the deception I object to. Why didn't you tell me?"

"But you met the art teacher, so you know."

"Know what? She's quite an artist herself, seems very pleasant, was delighted to have you."

"Yeah, but you *know.*" He was insistent.

"No, I don't *know.* What?"

"Mom, she's a negro."

"Yes. So?"

"Come on, Mom. You *know.*"

And suddenly a sick feeling rocked me. How can this happen? Who planted this ugly seed? "Kent, I'm going to tell you something important. By the time you are ten, you will not *see* or ever *think about* skin color. This is a promise!" Exactly how this condition was to be achieved, I was not sure.

I did find out that the lovely "Grandma" Stroud (no blood relation) who had since the beginning stayed with my children Monday through Friday while I taught school was unconsciously and quite innocently inculcated with the prejudice of her deep-south beginnings.

She and I had a talk on that very Saturday. She could not understand my position, nor could she agree; but she got my message on the subject where the children were concerned. And bless her heart, she tried very hard to avoid any future reference to the matter when the children were present—and for the most part, she succeeded.

And the **fourth** incident was more "a perfectly-timed opportunity." The Department of Interior posted a notice at my university that English teachers from the United States were wanted for the U.S. Trust Territory of the Pacific, a set of small islands called "Micronesia" in the West Pacific.

I was excited! *What* is Micronesia? Exactly *where* is Micronesia? They want English teachers from the U.S.? I'm one of those—and a *good* one, too! And my husband is *also* a teacher! Would he be willing to consider this opening? I picked up application papers (quite a packet!) and spent hours in the public library downtown to get answers to my questions, then discussed the matter at home. My husband was "willing to take a look."

Fine! I spent several evenings and a week end collecting and writing down information, mailed the application packet the next Monday morning. Oh boy!

The rest (as all too many people say) is *history.* Yes, we were selected, and yes, we went. And living suddenly on Venus could surely not involve greater change! I learned on the island of Saipan to distinguish between what is *necessary* to sustain life (very little) and what is clearly non-essential (all else). Here in this Pacific-washed dream world of a subtropical climate were a charming and gentle people with a dramatically different perception of practically everything. I believed then and I believe now that I was *born* on the island of Saipan at the age of thirty!

Some of the English teacher hires contracted a permanent case of "island fever"—too many dramatic changes occurring too soon in a too-small setting—so insisted on returning home immediately. But some families—and ours was one of these—thrived on the new life and managed to "nest" rapidly and comfortably. A magnificent bonus for some of us (certainly for Kent and me) was the underwater world here. With mask and snorkel, we rejoiced in the beauty of it, the teeming life below the surface, the adventure, the sheer *magnificence* of an alien and so-colorful cosmos unimagined heretofore.

I never thought I'd love swimming with sharks and octopuses. Nor did I ever suppose that a few small islands (we later moved to Pohnpei [then Ponape] where I worked for the University of Hawaii training indigenous teachers) and the Pacific Ocean would become my workplace *and* my playground. Yes, we returned to the U.S. when it was time for the children to attend junior high school. But the travel bug had bit hard. . . .

And so no, I never thought I'd be living in Thailand, after Kent and Karol were attending university. But there I was, working with International School Bangkok. And I learned in that place that a tonal Asian language is not SO hard to acquire when it means that one can leave the city and travel independently to smaller towns and swamps and jungles—and thereby *see* the offerings of the magical setting in which one lives.

I never thought that the proximity of Thailand to "other places" would provide opportunity to explore Nepal, Sumatra and Java, Sri Lanka, even Rangoon in Burma. Yes, *Kuala Lumpur* and *Kathmandu!* Not to mention "ordinary" trips to Hongkong and Singapore for shopping.

Nor did I ever think I'd be living and working in Italy at the American School of Milan . . . and visiting a stepdaughter who lived in Grenoble, France, along with her French husband and two children.

And while we're at it, I never thought I'd get to visit Africa, a long time yearning which—even though efforts to get *work* there never materialized—was satisfied when, following retirement after forty-five years as an educator and subsequent to being widowed, I did go spend three glorious weeks in Southern Africa—Zimbabwe and Botswana (and no, I never did meet the Ladies' #1 Detective)—and was amazed to discover that the safari-with-camera experience exceeded my most frenetic fantasies by about five hundred per cent.

So no, I never thought, back there in Nebraska, that I'd have these kinds of experiences. And Dr. Clark would be pleased to know that I now actually *do* have a few things to say. But a most satisfying aspect of this whole life trip is that both son Kent and daughter Karol are responsive to cultural differences . . . and truly impervious to skin color!

13

. . . .

Michener and Me

Long ago, my family and I, including a husband and two young children, planned to move to the West Pacific and (my husband and I) teach on the island of Saipan. For seven years, I'd been teaching composition and creative writing at a high school in Council Bluffs, Iowa, across the river from our home in Omaha. The *Nonpareil* (local newspaper) there sent a reporter to interview me one Sunday. My move was no big deal to Omaha, but was I guess "news" to much smaller Council Bluffs. I was relaxed because I knew the reporter—someone who sometimes substituted in English at "my" Thomas Jefferson High School.

However, when she asked if I planned to *write* out there, small lights in my brain twittered on and I answered very firmly, **"Yes. Letters!"**

No way to misunderstand that response, right? I was a bit sensitive because although I was considered an excellent *teacher* of writing, I had as yet published nothing but a few pieces in my university literary magazine—and those only while I served on that magazine staff, for heaven's sake. I very well *knew* that my own writing lacked style and polish. I did not yet even have a distinct *voice*. I flat out didn't write well, although I could recognize quality in the writing of others—including that of several students I had at the high school. So know right here that I was very firm in my response to the reporter: *Yes. Letters.*

The following Sunday—and I've often wished since that I had kept the article instead of crying all over it and ripping it into tiny pieces and flushing it—the gist of the huge spread boiled down (in my head then and now) to the following sentence:

> *. . . Mrs. Manning plans to do for the West Pacific what Michener has done for the South Pacific. . . .*

Say *what?* God in heaven! A big spread. Lots of great family pictures. But all I saw then and remember now were the words above. How could I face my students tomorrow? What about staff? How terribly, awfully, horribly embarrassing. I called the owner of the paper, a person whom I knew slightly, and demanded a retraction.

"Phyl, if I do that, everyone who paid no attention to the article the first time will pull that issue out of the trash bin and read every single word to see what we printed that wasn't true. Is that what you want?"

It wasn't.

Well, I DID get ribbed by students and staff. And I DID endure the banter by laughing it off. And we DID go to Saipan and—for some several years—lived in and traveled throughout the idyllic West Pacific. And although I DID NOT write anything other than letters while I was out there, I DID get to meet James Michener at a dinner party when he came through to visit some mutual friends on Saipan. He was not threatened by my proximity.

Later? Oh yes. Those years in the islands are a rich source for stories and articles and memoirs now that I have my craft fairly well in hand, my very own *voice,* a style developed, writing experience, some time and a bit of confidence.

Well, I've shared my anecdote. Do I need a moral? Okay: be very, very careful of the press. That reporter—for I confronted her on the matter the next time she subbed—never did see anything wrong with "turning our interview into a good story." *That's what reporters are supposed to do,* she told me. She actually believed that. I strongly disagreed then . . . and now.

14
· · · · · · · · · · · · · · · · · · · ·

(Sumatran Tiger)

The Queen of Roar

Nyla is miserable. Her nose is filled with a stinky stew of per-fume, after-shave lotion, and human sweat. Her ears ring with the shouts of strangers. And her sensitive eyes are dazzled by bright Hollywood sunshine reflecting off cameras and metal poles and other film equipment. Adding to her distress are peo-ple all around who are never still as they walk and sometimes run. She flattens her ears and growls a long, low rumble.

Nyla is young, a one-hundred-fifty-pound Sumatran tiger. Even as an adult, she will be smaller than her Bengal cousins. She will have brighter colors in her coat. And she will always be more restless. Bred, born and raised in captivity, Nyla has been trained for use in the film industry: "Put a tiger in your tank!" She is accustomed to people, yes. But not so *many* who are so *active* and so *noisy* and have such *unfamiliar smells*.

"It's a wrap!" booms out the sharp voice she's been hearing and hating for hours.

This has been a long, uncomfortable day spent shooting a commercial. The tiger is tired, frightened by everything. And as with people, a frightened cat may become an angry one. Nyla's growl turns into an ear-ripping roar . . . and over again.

"Shut her up!" shouts that same terrible voice. "Get her outta here!"

Nyla's trainer hurries forward to snap the leash onto her collar. But the tiger turns, claws his shoulder. She knocks him down and then pins him with her paw. Next she raises her handsome face and roars her displeasure. Her pain and frustration. What is a cat to do? Over and again, she roars until the mighty blasts take on a rhythm that brings to her a measure of comfort.

People gasp and scream, so there is more sound, more confusion, more distress.

The handler races in to take the leash. But he is met by those great curved fangs. He retreats, bleeding but not down. As he goes, he swoops his unhurt arm over to grab the trainer's good shoulder and drag him away.

"Some help here!" he shouts between the cat's roars. "Back that van in!" He tosses keys to a crew member. "**Do** it!"

Two husky men inch forward to help retrieve the bleeding trainer. For the cat, though, the next minutes are worse than everything previous during this dreadful day. Shouts and shrieks strike Nyla's ears. People dash to get away, push, fall. The tiger keeps roaring. Next comes a terrible wailing as an ambulance screams to a stop, doors slam open, men leap to pull out and raise two squeaking gurneys. Nyla roars more.

"Kill the siren!" someone says.

No one does. The whoops and groans continue, increasing ear pain for the cat. And so she keeps roaring.

Then she sees something familiar. Her travel cage is in the back of the open van. No one bars her way. She dashes over, leaps up and across the floor of the vehicle, then crouches into the familiar box. She trembles in terror. The van hatch slams shut, and Nyla feels safe. The unaccustomed smells and sounds and sights subside as she hears the siren fade away. Her own roars diminish to nervous growls and chuffs.

But later, her body still trembles as strangers move her cage to the home enclosure and cautiously open the gate. She cannot know that the two people she knows best—her trainer and her handler—are in the hospital now. She roars her displeasure at these unaccustomed people—at anyone who comes near.

"Heard about some trouble on the set, yesterday." Roberta Kirshner spoke by phone to a friend in the movie industry.

"You should believe it!" The words were emotionally charged. "Some tiger for a petroleum commercial? Mauled the trainer—but I hear he'll live. Handler was the lucky one—got only forty-six stitches."

"Whose animal? Where's the tiger now?"

The man told Roberta the owner's name. "Cat's probably put down. Not much choice—she's clawed human flesh, tasted human blood—"

"—Thanks, I'll call back," Roberta said.

She finally reached the holding company. Nyla still had a few hours to live, they reported. No one could get close enough to insert a needle, and the woman who owned the cat refused to let her be shot.

Then Roberta got through to the owner. "A Sumatran tiger—so beautiful!" the woman mourned. "She's always been hyper, ok? But she's smart and coachable, so the trainer and handler have told me."

"What happened on that set?" Roberta asked.

"Something. No one's talking." The woman sighed.

"I know this cat," Roberta said. She had seen the animal once as a cub, but mostly in TV commercials. "Don't put her down."

"—We train exotics for film, and you know that. Now Nylas's barred from every set—won't ever be trusted again. We can't afford to keep useless animals—"

"—Don't euthanize! I'll take her. Can you send her up?" To get that rare and beautiful creature, Roberta would have made the thousand-plus round trip miles from Northern to Southern California and back by crawling on her hands and knees. But the owner seemed to have a soft spot for Nyla . . . and her corporation was bound to have more money than Roberta to apply toward transportation.

At first, silence. Then the owner continued. "She's seriously agitated, you know. No one can get close. Food has to go to her on a pole. Water—we just aim a hose at the bowl."

Roberta knew that the big cat had been frightened, had reverted to its wild nature. It was the trainer's job, and the handler's, to stay sensitive minute by minute to mood. And Sumatran tigers are *moody*, no mistake. They are a nervous subspecies, quick to react and slow to adjust to change. That disaster on the set wasn't Nyla's fault. It shouldn't have happened. "She still deserves a good quality of life," Roberta said softly.

Did the owner hear her? "All that cat does now is roar! She'll upset your other animals."

"I'll re-train her." Roberta's voice was calm and certain.

"Pardon me—but I seriously doubt that." The woman surely knew Roberta Kirshner's reputation—Director and Owner of Kirshner Wildlife Foundation located up north near Chico. But this young cat had always been tightly wound. The recent experience had unraveled her totally and perhaps permanently.

Still, Roberta must have given the owner hope, for the woman's sigh could be heard across the line. "Ok, I'll get her to you."

So Nyla and her marrow-churning roar came to Northern California. Roberta spent almost a year of spare and not-so-spare time sitting outside the cat's enclosure for hours of every day and especially night. There, she talked to Nyla and read aloud and played music (Nyla prefers country western). Finally, this long-experienced trainer dared to enter the tiger's cage so that fresh instruction could begin.

That was ten years ago. Now, through Roberta's patience and knowhow and special magic, Nyla is fully trained—as dependable as a big cat *can* be. She is docile when she wears a collar and leash to go out to schools and community events as an ambassador for the Foundation. There, she carries the compelling message about preserving wildlife and habitat. But Roberta watches carefully for any sign of restlessness when the cat is off site.

Today, at her 350-pound adult weight, this Sumatran tiger is smaller than the more familiar Bengal subspecies, much smaller than Siberians. She has brilliant striping—burnished orange, jet black, a glow of pale ivory accents. Drastically endangered, fewer than two hundred Sumatrans remain on this planet, and these are mostly in captivity. No wonder they're nervous.

Nyla still has a short fuse. She expresses anger (fear) with sustained, ear-blasting roars. Recently, the California Conservation Corps arrived at the Foundation to help spruce things up. Fifteen young men and women wore uniforms and—shimmering in bright sunlight—neon blue plastic hard hats.

Nyla didn't know these people, and she didn't like their looks. She roared her objection, and kept *on* roaring. After a quarter hour of sustained sound, Roberta suggested—loudly, above the tiger's decibels—that corps members might want to take off their shiny hats. They did, and the cat quieted immediately. Next morning, when several forgot and wore their headgear, Nyla tuned up again right away. The few sheepishly removed the offending article and were relieved by the tiger's sudden silence.

Yesterday, the thermometer registered over a hundred degrees. Roberta tossed keys for the outer fence to one of her volunteers: me. She suggested that I first hose down the big white Bengal-Siberian hybrid named Chuffy. "Then do Nyla." Tigers like to be cool. Those in the wild which live in tropical climates spend much of each hot summer trying to chill off in a river or lake or in deep forest shade. Chuffy is a mellow tiger—a 500-pound pussycat—who gently plays with the much smaller Nyla when the two are turned together in an outer pen. Nyla acknowledges Chuffy's superior size and strength, so interacts amicably.

As instructed, and of course standing outside the barred inner enclosure, I hosed Chuffy first. Nyla knows and accepts me and certain other volunteers—so long as we don't change body powder or wear earrings or do some other darn fool thing to annoy her.

When it was Nyla's turn, I approached the Sumatran's enclosure with a hose having a pistol grip. "Onto the deck!" I told her. That wooden deck prevents the rest of the cage from turning into a bog at cool-off time.

But well in front of the platform, Nyla stretched out in the dirt-and-sawdust bedding. Her golden eyes were fastened on me. She knew absolutely that no cooling gush of water would come to her here. Nyla was teasing and testing.

"The *deck,* pretty kitty." I sent a stream of water beyond the cat to wet down the boards on the low platform behind her. Nyla turned her head to see the damp surface, then turned back without getting up, eyed me.

"Get on the *deck,* baby."

Nyla stood up, turned a full circle, then flopped back down right where she'd been.

She thought I was blind? "Ok, then." I released the grip, returned to Chuffy with the hose.

Nyla roared. I turned back.

Nyla stepped up onto the platform and lay down belly up, stretching both front paws above her head. If she could speak, her words would have been, "Get the pits first, ok?"

The hose drenched her forelegs and stomach. She stretched her back legs, and I obliged. The cat rolled over, and I sprayed her shoulders, flanks and backside—careful not to dampen ears or eyes. That, no tiger likes.

The spray stopped when I relaxed my fingers from the grip in order to stretch them.

Nyla roared, came steaming from her deck to lunge high and spread-eagle against the cyclone fencing.

"Hey, you've had plenty," I told her.

Back to the boards Nyla leapt, then slapped herself flat for more wetting.

So I changed hands on the hose, spattered the prone tiger for another five minutes.

"Enough. Definitely." I released the trigger.

This time, Nyla let her shower cease without protest. And why not? She had, after all, made her point. . . .

15

(Big Ears & Long Legs)

The B. E. L. L. Cats

Overhead, clouds scud across a near-full moon. Shadows sweep the rough landscape. A furry bundle with long ears moves out on arid ground—hesitant, this rabbit, a pause between each timid hop.

Now a dark shape separates silently from the umbra of a boulder and leaps in a graceful arc to attack its prey without the barely audible sounds of a stalk, then rolls, clutching and kicking to secure and finally to enjoy its meal.

This dark shape is the caracal, a middle-sized hunting cat which gets its name from the Turkish word *karakulak,* meaning "black ears." That Turks contributed the name suggests that this cat most closely linked to Africa today is found elsewhere also, or at least was in Turkey at one time.

In fact, the caracal enjoys a wider range than any exotic *felid* other than the leopard. Caracals are present—albeit in decreasing numbers—throughout wild and rocky terrain in Western Asia and the Near East, desert perimeters of Arab lands and the North African Sahara and even rough land in Southeastern Europe, notably Greece. The handsome but fierce creature can also be located in central and sub-equatorial Africa including edges of the Kalahari.

The black ears of a caracal have tufts; and these cats therefore are considered close kin to other tuft-ear cats, notably lynxes and bobcats. But in habitat and habits, the caracal is more comparable to the serval—another mid-sized cat, this one found only in sub-Sahara Africa.

Not that they look alike, other than both being *"bell* cats" having **big** **e**ars and **l**ong **l**egs. But let's watch one serval do what she does best—hunt.

It's very late in the day, but that same storm is blowing through—lots of wind rippling long grasses and churning up whitecaps on a nearby waterway. Those same ragged clouds scud along the western horizon in the last crimson purples of sunset.

A spotted, medium-sized cat crouches in fluttering grass and blends perfectly in the gleam and gloom of a troubled twilight. Intent on the surroundings, her huge ears twist independently in any direction to attend a rustle not in synch with the wind.

Diurnal creatures are bedding for the night; nocturnal ones are stirring. And the mainly crepuscular serval is alert, waiting, listening, looking without moving.

For whatever reason, perhaps a marauding mamba, there bursts frantically from the branches of an acacia tree a flurry of noisy, lilac-breasted rollers. The serval leaps up twelve feet into the air, pivoting as she goes, one sharp claw swiping in one direction, another stretching in counterpoint. Two fowl come crashing down. The serval spins on her return to earth and bats yet another bird from the sky, all faster than any eye can follow.

The spotted cat hits the ground gracefully, hurrying to finish off her three victims with a single bite to the neck of each, then *chirtles* for her twin kittens to come from hiding and join the feast.

Do you see similarity in these silent hunters? Both serval and caracal lie in wait, stalk, pounce, or leap-and-swipe, according to prey and circumstance. Both are quick enough to snatch their meal off the wing, bold enough to attack whole families of raptors in their large nest atop a cliff or tree. With hind legs especially long, both can sprint to capture small antelope. Basically carnivores, both enjoy guinea fowl, unwary hares and monkeys, rodents and hyraxes . . . or will settle for insects, even berries and other fruit if absolutely necessary.

Some other physical ways in which these two *bell* cats resemble each other include triple duty for those king-sized ears. A serval is sometimes described as "bat-eared," whereas a caracal has those tufted ears which aid in camouflage when he walks through dry grasses. But the wolf who ate Grandma had it right when he told Red that those big ears of his were "all the better to *hear* you with."

Most cats favor smell and sight to pinpoint prey, leaving the acute sense of hearing to their canine kin. But serval and caracal have energetic, "tracking" ears that can be positioned independently to pick up subtle nuances that include a tunneling mole or a scuttling lizard. The position and movement of those ears also communicate to others of their kind the mood of their owner. Sufficiently angered with ears flattened against the skull, a caracal appears to have no ears at all. And finally, as is true of elephants, the big ears of both these cats serve as a cooling system for circulating blood on a hot day in the torrid places where they live.

Yes, other similarities exist. Both b.e.l.l. cats have smallish heads when compared to body size. Both have pointed muzzles furred white to ivory. Both have extraordinarily long, very muscular hind legs. And unlike many other cats, serval and caracal tails are thick but of only medium length—substantial enough to be useful with balance when the cats leap but not long enough to get in the way.

And both the serval and the caracal qualify as "small cats" because they have hyoid bones attached on both sides—meaning that they can purr without effort but lack the vibrato to chuff or roar.

In fact, the greatest *contrast* between servals and caracals lies in coat texture and coloration, and also in disposition. The serval coat is a somewhat bristly yellowed ivory and so densely spotted longitudinally with dark chocolate that the markings may join to form lines, especially at the haunch and neck. As is true for leopard, jaguar and ocelot as well as for much smaller spotted cats in the wild, these markings blend well with the sun and shadow of veldt and riverine woodland that a serval favors.

Some say that the caracal (also known as the African wildcat) wears a brown tuxedo. Again, though, this near-monochromatic coloration blends with the rough ground and rocky terrain and sand favored by caracals.

Although both animals are two to three feet in length without the tail, and both are about one and a half feet high to the shoulder, caracals are built more densely. Where a healthy adult male serval weighs in around thirty-to-forty pounds, the caracal of similar age, health, and gender will be perhaps ten pounds heavier.

In temperament, too, the animals differ. A serval in the wild tends to be more mellow, non-confrontational. This cat will freeze or conceal itself . . . get away if possible rather than face some larger, unknown and possibly fiercer creature. Caracals are more aggressive. They have been known to attack and do serious damage even to humans invading their territory.

And although a caracal is neatly identified on the evolutionary ladder, scientists are only recently and hesitantly beginning to identify the lineage of the serval (along with the diminutive "rusty-spot" cat of India and Sri Lanka).

The caracal, unlike the serval, is one of several "small" cats to break the rule by having eye pupils that contract when relaxed to a circle rather than a spindle. That's supposed to be a "big" cat trait.

There was a time when a caracal or two were kept well fed in wealthy Persian and Indian households as hunters. The creatures could be used to chase down birds and antelope—their natural prey. This training consisted of teaching the caracal *not* to attack the person holding its harness leash and *not* to devour immediately whatever it caught—but rather wait for the human hunter to dress the prey and reward the caracal with delectable tidbits.

But there is no record found so far that caracals were ever actually gentled like cheetahs and kept other than in secure enclosures whenever not fastened to a lead chain in the field. And no picture, oral history or written record suggests that servals were *ever* part of human households for any reason.

But then, people living in serval territory (southern Africa) were mostly migratory until recent times. And probably these wilderness-savvy folk knew what others have had to learn the hard way over centuries—that the carnivores around them— and with few exceptions—can be trained but never truly tamed.

16

(The White Bengal with Gene-Pool Problems)

Sean the Survivor

The red-haired woman thanks the flight attendant and grasps the warm nursing bottle, then walks back to her seat—actually, to her three seats straight out from the window in the half-filled red-eye flight east to west, she should always be so lucky!

Roberta Kirshner lifts the bright tapestry carryall from the middle seat and places it gently onto her lap as she sits down. She studies the aisle carefully, up and down. No one about. She allows two drops of white liquid to fall onto her forearm. Warm enough, not too hot. Now she opens the bag and pushes her wallet and cosmetic pouch off to the side.

"Hey, little guy." Her right hand drops into the opening to pet the soft, furry head. "Ready for food?"

The response is a twitter of discontent—*I'm here. I'm hungry.* A baby's message that transcends species.

She lowers the bottle into the bag and inserts the nipple into the small pink mouth of the waiting infant. His tongue curls around the rubber teat. Sucking sounds.

"Whoa, not so much noise!" Roberta whispers. "They'll throw us off without a parachute." She looks out the window into blackness. "Probably somewhere over the Central Plains, and a long walk home."

Roberta hums aloud to cover the sounds of greed. But then the bottle is empty and the baby asleep. Nothing this hungry, the woman keeps telling herself, can be as bad off as that breeder has told her. So the cub *is* what's (called erroneously) "lactose intolerant"—but really a matter of not handling the proteins in cow's milk? Well, neither can a lot of human babies; but for merely that, no one gives up on a *Homo sapiens* kid. We don't put *them* to sleep permanently. Besides, Roberta's quick fix—combined acidophilus and goat milk—seems to be working.

But now what about the gazillion other problems belonging to this tiny tiger? The bumping into things when he toddles around? The falling down? The general clumsiness, so *un*tiger-like. A tiger is the ballerina among felines—fluid in movement, always graceful. And those seizures—he's already had a couple today. Once he even lost consciousness. Why does he suddenly tighten up and start shaking? Then afterward, he seems so dazed—as if he's just crash-landed in from the Milky Way.

Well, come on. . . . Give herself *time*. She needs to observe him more than these barely seven hours she's been with him so far.

"Is he asleep? Could I see?" The flight attendant who has heated bottles three times so far during the trip displays the name "Judy" across her silver wings. She puts a knee against the aisle armrest and leans over to look into the slightly open carryall.

"Oh!" She pulls back in surprise, a small frown marring otherwise placid features, her eyes suddenly on her passenger.

Roberta waggles both eyebrows and shrugs. "As you know, this baby needs formula every couple of hours." She grins. "Sometimes oftener."

"Oh." Judy bends back over to take another look. "May I?" A beautifully manicured left hand hovers over the opening of the bag.

Roberta thinks fast. She is not enthusiastic about having the woman's hand on the infant's head—who *knows* where that hand has been? But even less appealing is the idea of forcing this seven-pound baby into quarantine at someplace on board inaccessible to Roberta. Oh, the cat is entirely legal. All the paperwork is completed and at her fingertips, right here in the bag. No small feat, either. Where wildlife is concerned, California has the toughest restrictions in the country. But this month-old infant is supposed to be traveling air cargo. Roberta knows that the delicate tiger child will not survive a five-hour flight without hands-on care and a warmed bottle at approximately two-hour intervals.

So Roberta nods with as much animation as she can muster. How can Judy possibly resist the needs of the tiny traveler after she touches his velvet head? After she looks into those appealing blue eyes?

"Oh-hh!" Judy has slid into the aisle seat, and both her hands are now at the opening flap of the carryall. "May I—can I please take it out?"

Roberta shakes her head, trying not to show her alarm. "Maybe later—after he wakes up, ok?"

The flight attendant nods. A broad smile stretches across her face as she gets up from the seat. "Of course!" she agrees. "I shouldn't even have asked."

Roberta offers the woman her papers including the California permit. Judy barely glances at them. But already in flight, what could she actually *do?* For this woman, Roberta decides, a baby is a baby is a baby.

Almost two hours later, the cat awakens with a *twitter*—nothing human, certainly, but not feline, either. A fluttery *cheeping* in an upper register that carries. This baby in his flowery cradle wants food. Now.

Judy hurries down the aisle from the forward galley just as Roberta pulls out another prepared bottle. She sighs as she glances out the window at first dawn on snowy mountains. The Sierras, have to be. She has only one additional bottle remaining. It must be saved for the ride home after deplaning. Who could have guessed how hungry this little guy would be?

Passengers are craning their necks to see what has made the sound. All business, Judy marches to the forward galley as if warming bottles for wildlife specimens is part of her normal service. Her return with the sturdy plastic container, though, are like tossing a big stone into a small pond: circles kept widening. People behind Roberta half-stand to peer into the now-noisy receptacle on her lap. Those across the aisle have a ringside seat, and they use it.

One youngster at the window seat in front of her gets onto his knees, belly-to-buttons. He not only hangs over the back of the seat but also gives a running monologue in sport-announcer volume that carries throughout the coach section.

"She got somethin' in the bag—somethin' takes a bottle, ok?"

The boy's shrill tones alarm the infant, who then emits sustained birdlike chirps.

"Somethin' weird, all right."

Judy slides slickly into the aisle seat. "May I?"

Roberta nods. Why not? She shakes her head at the boy draped across the seat-back before her. No response. When she looks back, Judy has taken the cat from the carryall and settled him into the crook of her arm. She places the nipple between eager pink lips. The woman has given literal meaning to *letting the cat out of the bag.*

Not that the cub minds. His eyes are clenched in bliss, his paws kneading air on either side of the container, his lips sucking noisily.

"It's a *tiger!*" the boy announces with vociferous triumph. "Stripes an' everything—only it's **white** —a baby white tiger!" Then, in echoing awe, he adds, "With browny-pink stripes, though."

The passengers cannot resist coming to take a look. They are orderly but determined, Roberta reflects as they file past over and again. Most can't resist touching the soft fur, but all are gentle. No one expresses alarm—least of all the baby, now finished with his meal and content but too aware of his admirers to fall asleep. He absorbs attention as his just due, and Roberta relaxes, puts away her fear of germs because there is no way to stop the curious people.

Nothing seems to alarm the cat. He finally emits a soft belch and can no longer keep his eyes open. Judy stands to whisk a folded blanket from somewhere overhead. She lays the tiger on it at the aisle seat where she's been sitting. Roberta puts her carryall over to the window and is grateful to get the extra pounds off her lap.

"You got any more of those in there, lady?" the boy wants to know.

She chuckles, shakes her head. "But lots bigger ones at home." She'd let the young man chew on that information for a while. Roberta operates a wildlife foundation that protects mostly endangered species and goes out to educate the community. She has more than a hundred animals awaiting her return.

The youngster manages to trade seats with one of his parents and spends the remainder of the trip blessedly quiet as he hangs over the back of the aisle seat to watch the tiger sleep.

While the plane makes its long descent coming into Sacramento, Judy takes the one remaining bottle from Roberta, heats it extra-warm, then wraps it in paper toweling. "You have quite a ways to go beyond the airport?" she asks.

"About eighty miles straight north," Roberta says. "My van's in long term parking."

"Need some help with luggage?"

The older woman chucks her chin at the seat-belted bag beside her. "All here. Quick trip."

Judy nods. "Suppose we'd better tuck him in for the landing." She slides her hands under the blanket while Roberta unzips the carryall.

The two women ease the still-sleeping infant with the blanket toward the bag.

"Now if you need other help, you let me know," Judy tells her.

"Me, too!" added the boy. "I can do lots of stuff!" Now he plunges precariously closer across the back of the seat. "Let me hold the bag open!"

Judy pulls back the blanket, then steadies the boy to keep him from over-balancing. Still without awakening the baby, Roberta eases him once again into the opening which the boy is using both hands to keep wide.

The plane lands, but when the seatbelt lights go off, none of the cabin passengers move. Someone starts clapping. Then everyone—softly, rhythmically in unison.

Judy smiles and leans over to Roberta's ear. "They want you to get off first," she says. Then adds, "It's an honor."

Roberta is embarrassed but can't help being pleased. She's never heard of such a thing, but there is no time to argue the matter. She would much prefer to simply go out with the other passengers, then immediately take a quick detour to the parking lot and retrieve the small carrier from the hatch of her van—and finally take herself to the cargo gate and present papers and one small properly-caged, striped cat. Her preference—but now not possible.

She'll have to play it their way. And this she does. She realizes later that she hadn't fooled anyone—not on the plane, certainly. Nor at the airport. She also realized that everyone has been on *her* side—hers and that of the tiger cub.

Other animals at the wildlife shelter required her time when she got home. But the newcomer wanted and needed it *all*. Seriously sleep deprived, Roberta sought help from nearby California State University at Chico. Students from animal science programs came out on four-hour shifts around the clock to feed and reassure and give affection to the small white tiger.

Within a week, Roberta had tentatively diagnosed the main problems. After a month, she took the baby for testing to an animal medical center near Sacramento. Veterinarians there put the two-month-old through a series of tests. After a second round of evaluations they decided he—like a good many human infants—was allergic to cow's milk. That he had some kind of stomach disorder which affected his metabolizing at least calcium—hence the intermittent limping. They noted that he had seizures. And that he probably had a "serious sight deficiency."

Now, did Roberta wish to have an ophthalmologist assess the exact amount of sight remaining? They had someone who would test without charge, just for the experience. In fact, someone who *wanted* to do the analysis.

None of the center's findings were news to Roberta. Herself skilled in veterinary medicine and having many decades of experience with wildlife and especially with the exotic cats, she had figured it out in that first week. And she already knew how much eyesight the cub had—*very little.*

But the procedure of measuring visual acuity in a tiger intrigued her, so she agreed. The process was interesting, the results specific. The cub had 17% vision in his left eye, 20% in his right. The tiny muscles responsible for focusing were atrophied.

"Not much to be done for this little guy," the reporting doctor said with regret in his voice. "Another gene pool victim—way too many recessive genes paired up. Breeder should've had DNA testing on both parents before they were bred."

Roberta nodded. "And DNA testing shouldn't cost over a thousand dollars each for the exotic cats," she said. Especially when it cost only fifty dollars for a horse. So only the very wealthiest wildlife centers could afford the DNA check absolutely necessary for responsible breeding of endangered species having such severely diminished gene pools. That's why Roberta doesn't do breeding.

"So too many problems. He can't live long—just make him comfortable as possible, I suppose. Nothing else to do." Those were the words of the university vet.

Roberta fought tears. "He lives in my house—sleeps on my bed in his own blanket."

The vet raised his eyebrows. "Now that's *comfortable,*" he commented. "But to deal with the lack of vision we do have suggestions. If he has an enclosure—I mean, if he lives long enough to need one—then you'll want to wrap the perimeter with carpeting."

Roberta didn't think so. "He'd *eat* it! Choke."

The man shrugged. "Otherwise, he'll always be bruised—likely, ultimately, *literally* break his neck."

Roberta didn't comment, but paid her sizable bill for medical services. All the way home, the little one asleep on the seat beside her, his head on her lap, she considered means to alert that cat to territory boundaries without closing him in. A long car trip was a good time for thinking.

When the two got into the house, Roberta placed the tiny tiger onto the kitchen floor, then headed for the bathroom medicine cabinet. She took out a large jar of Vick's Vaporub from the shelf, opened it and rubbed it onto the lower reaches of the refrigerator. She looked around, then rubbed it on both sides of the sliding door going outside. Again on the lower cupboards, table legs.

"Don't use much," she counseled herself. "No olfactory difficulties that we know of." Yeah, but everything else wrong possible, a desolate voice inside her piped up.

Then she squared her shoulders. "Uh-huh. And diet plus vitamin injections and TLC with careful training will take care of most problems." Roberta put back the jar of jelly, then picked up her cub.

"Baby, I have great ideas," she told him. "You're going to get healthy—grow up just fine and live a long and happy life."

A month later, one visitor at Kirshner Wildlife asked the name of the small white tiger in Roberta's arms.

Roberta realized suddenly that the cub was referred to by her and all the volunteers only as "the baby." She turned to an intern who worked cats under Roberta's supervision.

"Sean," she said to him. "What do you think should be—"

"—*Sean!*" cooed the visitor. "What a perfect name for such a lovable kitty."

It would have been easy to drop that unlikely appellation when the woman drove down the driveway. But the name stuck.

Today, Sean is almost five years old and weighs a whopping five hundred pounds. He has his own enclosure, aromatic at the perimeters with Vaporub and cloves. He has not had a full seizure in almost two years, and he only limps when it rains. He lacks the motor coordination (or possibly the inclination) to clean himself with that rasping tiger tongue. Tipping his water pail and rolling in the muck it creates is one of his favorite pastimes. In cold weather, when one cannot safely shower him down with a hose, he tends to resemble a mudball. Also, he still can't see much more than shadows, still can't focus on even *those,* and of course is therefore without depth perception.

But on a collar and leash, he knows that two tugs mean "Step up" and one tug, "Down." He gets along quite well. In fact, he goes out as an ambassador for the Kirshner Wildlife Foundation to help emphasize the need for conservation of wildlife and habitat. He has participated in over three hundred educational programs and personal contacts with youngsters who are ill. The Make-a-Wish Foundation and The Ronald MacDonald House bring their ailing children to interact with the mellow and healthy, well-trained animals on the preserve near Chico in Northern California.

Or Sean goes to hospitals or private homes where (when still small) he would clamber up onto a couch or bed and *cuddle* with an ailing child. Nothing is wrong with Sean's heart or sense of compassion.

So yes, it would have been better had DNA testing taken place. But given the *fact* of Sean, his situation is the best possible. He is well cared for and much loved. Roberta shows how he has compensated for if not entirely cured his original difficulties. As for size and appearance—he's a large animal, even for a Siberian/Bengal mix.

Still lacking that typical "cat" habit of meticulous grooming, he remains dependent on Roberta's ministrations with water and scrub-brush. Except when muddied, he's white with a rich, glossy coat and cinnamon stripes.

Roberta Kirshner believes him likely to live out the full dozen to fifteen years of average tiger "longevity," perhaps the twenty-year expectation for tigers in captivity. But his friends throughout the region—and these are many—expect Sean to live forever.

17

· · · · · · · · · · · · · · · · · · ·

(African Lioness)

Angelpuss

Roberta Kirshner rents a car after the plane lands in Kansas City. Her nephew Billy insists on carrying the one bag they brought. He is fourteen, flame-haired, freckle-faced and frowning.

"What I don't get is how come we go to Kansas to get an African lion," he complains.

Roberta snorts. She'd bet bucks—if she were a betting woman—that he'd thought the two of them were headed for Africa when they left the wildlife foundation near Chico. In fact, so sure that he'd not even asked. She chuckled.

"Owners and trainers pay me for information. Sometimes, I take that pay in animal trade."

"Instead of money." His tone suggests that he's not sold on the idea.

"Good healthy wildlife costs a lot, Billy. And some of our most prized animals at the Foundation are there in lieu of consultation fees."

"Consultation." Billy picked up a telephone call from Japan on Roberta's phone yesterday. And then a couple of days ago, he'd answered one call for his aunt from India and another from Australia. "People from overseas ask you questions?"

"From here in the U.S., too. About nutrition, for some new or ailing animal—or about behavior—my two specialties in the wildlife department." After a moment, "Often about cats." Thank goodness, she thinks.

Roberta Kirshner loves cats—their beauty, power, intelligence, everything about them. Her wildlife foundation has leopards, servals, caracals, ocelots, a lynx and a bobcat, along with some magnificent tigers—but no lion, as Billy has reminded her all summer, during his visit. Neither the big African nor the smaller Asian from the Gir Forest in northwest India.

"So now we're getting an African lion cub from Kansas instead of someone paying you money." Billy's tone is still skeptical, and Roberta has to smile.

"We?" His aunt chuckles. The boy likes money. He knows that air travel to Africa costs a lot—may have even checked it out on line with his laptop—but Africa is where he would like to have them go. He's made that fact very plain.

"So someone in Kansas owes you a *consultation* fee?" he asks now.

"Big time."

Roberta knows he thinks she should take the money instead of a Kansas lion, then apply it toward his longed-for trip to Africa. But he's not likely to voice that thought, she believes, for he knows very well that it's her money and her decision. What Billy does not yet know is that the few remaining wild lions in the world need to be left in the wild. But he'll get the whole picture, one of these days.

Roberta fastens her seatbelt, waits for him to do likewise, then drives out of the car rental lot to go west into Kansas. "We'll get a brand new baby—pick of the litter, and I know this litter. I once worked where we're going, Billy—well before starting the Foundation."

"Wouldn't you be better off to take the mother, then, since you two already know each other?"

"The mother was getting old. She died three days ago."

"So these are orphans! That's why the cubs are available right now?"

Roberta nods her own red curls, glances over at her nephew. "And when we get back, you'll help me with bottle feeding, right?"

Billy nods automatically. Every three hours. He knows the drill. That should be interesting—but not as exciting as a trip to Africa in search of a baby lion. . . .

Roberta is tired, and Billy is restless. For nearly two full days, they have been here at this Kansas preserve to observe the same three lion cubs in their large enclosure. The woman suspects that the owner is getting impatient, as well. He comes over to them with fair frequency. But instead of looking at the animals, he narrows his eyes to observe Roberta. He hasn't said much.

Other visitors are milling around, too. Roberta recognizes and speaks to some of them.

"These are mostly knowledgeable people," she tells Billy, "representing wildlife shelters of various kinds, breeding facilities, even a few zoos."

Several people must be interested in these particular cubs because they stand nearby until the owner shoos them away, explaining that the woman with auburn hair has first choice.

Roberta grins on hearing him say this, is holding back her excitement. She has earned the right to take her pick of any lion litter at this large facility, right? And her foundation back home "needs" one, as Billy has pointed out throughout his summer stay.

And she is so fortunate to get a cub from the issue of the lioness she once knew so well: pure African stock for size, health and heft. One of these chubby beauties. *Which?*

Actually, Roberta Kirshner knows most captive-bred lion bloodlines in the United States and to some extent in the world. She knows a great deal about lions . . . about Big Cats . . . about all cats . . . about wildlife in general. And why not? She was raised around animals by parents and also grandparents on both sides who trained animals for the film industry. She has handled wildlife since before her tenth birthday.

A youngster, Roberta helped with handling animals backstage in the shooting of several *Tarzan* films. And as a teenager skilled in equitation, she stood in on the "rough" riding for young film stars doing those Westerns so popular in the '50's and '60's, including Natalie Wood and Shirley MacLaine when their script called for the horse they were riding to come up against a rattlesnake or a mountain lion, even a grizzly.

But which cub? All three look similar, and all are females. Two are friendly and lovable. One is not. And these qualities were evident in the first fifteen minutes after they arrived. What is she waiting for? She intently watches and watches . . . and the hours pass. . . . She is weighing factors from within a strange dilemma. Shall she be lazy, take the "easy" way? Or shall she take an opportunity to exercise skill she knows she has?

"What are you hoping to see?" Billy finally asks.

"Health, of course," she tells him. "Intelligence, personality. And spirit."

Well, the three cubs are littermates and three weeks old—older than the woman would prefer to have them when they first come to her. All have the same rough, tawny coats, similar chocolate freckles and golden eyes—beautiful! All seem equally healthy and energetic, similarly alert.

Roberta thinks that Billy is probably relieved in knowledge that his opinion will not weigh into the choice. After all, it is she herself who must live for years with the result.

"You don't select an animal with your eyes or even your brain, Billy. You do it with your intuition—with your *heart.*" And therein lies Roberta's problem.

Certainly she knows which cub Billy prefers in particular. She is docile, affectionate. She not only lets him pet her but deliberately rubs up under his hand for attention. And Roberta knows which cub he probably likes least—for she's a real terror.

Loud, quarrelsome with her sisters. Big trouble on four stubby legs! At this moment, the ornery one is playing Queen of the Mountain with the bits of dried meat kibble in the bowl. Her little stomach distended from eating all that she could and more than she should, this ferocious little lioness now stands with hind legs adrift in food and both forelegs in front of the bowl. She shifts her weight from one foot to the other, both equally ready to swat any sister who dares come close.

The Queen's muzzle is wrinkled, lips drawn back. A sustained growl issues from between bared little needle teeth. She means business. Billy glances up at his aunt, sees that she is frowning thoughtfully.

The breeder has walked up, is watching the Queen's display. He taps Roberta on the arm. "She's a surly one—same litter, but a monster. Happens, sometimes."

The man sounds apologetic—as if *he* were the selfish one or at least somehow responsible for her behavior.

Then he continues. "Shall I just take her out of the enclosure?

"Leave her," Roberta tells him without letting her eyes exit the scene as the two hungry cubs approach the food dish. The tyrant ensconced there sends the first one sprawling, and the remaining cub turns away. She walks over pretending to examine the mesh of the enclosure while she waits for her sister's attention to wander. Then she creeps in for a nibble off the back of the bowl but is defeated immediately when the despot hears a crunch. Roberta laughs aloud.

"How can we account for such a large difference in personality among cats who carry the same genes?" she wonders aloud to her nephew. And she *knows* these genes! Not that many years back, at this very wildlife site, she trained these cubs' mother and *her* mother before that—both spectacular lionesses, the older one brought over from Africa. Both were bright and sometimes even cooperative ladies. Roberta had met the sires, too, had studied DNA results before breeding could be permitted.

Other buyers are waiting for lions and eager for her to choose . . . like Roberta, these are savvy people representing zoos and wildlife shelters of various kinds—some of them experts familiar with this particular line.

"Pick!" Roberta tells herself. "Choose one, and be done with it." More easily thought than accomplished.

Among the Big Cats, lions are toughest. Not most vicious—leopards can be wily killers who seem sometimes to take prey without regard for hunger. Lions aren't biggest, either, even the African ones—for tigers are the longest, highest at the haunch and heaviest cats on the planet. But in face-to-face combat, who would win?

First, no tiger—which is an Asian animal, not African— has ever met the big African lion or lioness in the wild, at least not in historical record. They live for the most part on different continents.

Big & Small Cats

The thirty-seven species of cats in the wild are divided by many scientists among "Big Cats" (7) and "Small Cats"(30). This division is based (arguably) not so much on size as—are you ready for this?—on differences in the voice box. For example, the Western Cougar (also called by such names as *puma, panther, mountain lion, painter* and *catamount)* is considered a Small Cat even though it may be half again the size of a "Big Cat" leopard.

Experts disagree about the basis for classification. Big Cat eyes usually have round pupils where Small Cat eye pupils are usually spindle-shaped. But not always.

A main difference most agree on is that Big Cats can roar but are unable to purr non-stop. They *can* and sometimes do make a similar but louder sound (called "chuffing") but only on exhaling. This fact is no reflection on their temperament. And Small Cats are just the opposite—they can purr without effort and forever, inhaling and exhaling, from pleasure, pain or stress—but cannot roar.

Reason? The hyoid bone at the larynx (voice box) in Big Cats is not fully joined. The hyoid *is* joined for what are classified as Small Cats—as it is for humans and all other animals having a larynx.

This "looseness" allows Big Cats vibration and volume resulting in a roar which—for tigers and lions, at least—can be heard five miles away. That unconnected hyoid, as indicated above, also permits that expressive "chuff" sound that is more than a purr but not a growl, something which can be positive or negative or sexual.

All cats can and will flatten their ears, hiss, spit and growl—but it's the roaring and chuffing as contrasted with purring that make the big difference for Big Cat/Small Cat classification.

Still, just to show how inconsistent even scientists can be, cheetahs and clouded leopards as well as snow leopards—all three of which have fully connected hyoids, so *cannot* roar or chuff—seem to be classified as Big Cats along with the roarers and chuffers, mainly tigers, lions, leopards and jaguars.

Are we confused yet? But Roberta is certain that the lion would triumph in a contest of strength and ferocity. Why?

The tiger is a single cub, occasionally a twin, an animal with the full protection, attention and affection of its mother. All tigers live alone in the wild, a single adult or a mother with her cub(s).

But the lion cub is only one in a litter so large that it often exceeds the teats on the mother. So from the very beginning, a lion must *compete* . . . at first by matching wits with brothers and sisters for "a place at the table" and soon with all other cubs of the pride into which it has been born. The mortality rate on lion cubs in their natural environment is high for one reason: starvation.

At a kill, the lions eat first, the lionesses next. And finally, the cubs share whatever may remain—not much, usually, and that little will be enjoyed by only the most aggressive among the youngsters.

So from the very start, a lion cub has to be first and fierce to get food. Those least pushy go hungry and ultimately die. So a strike-first attitude seems to be built into lions and lionesses, even those born in captivity, where all animals are dependably well fed. Competition and aggression seems to be in the genes.

Yes, Roberta is quite sure that a lion would win over a tiger in any struggle. And she *knows* from long experience that lions are the more difficult to educate.

She tries to get animals, and especially the fierce cats, when they are very young—a few days or at most a few weeks old. Then she can begin simple training early—hands-on tolerance and the "no bite" command—while the youngsters bond with her first as their affectionate parent who feeds and cuddles them and later as their boss. But this relationship is never simple with a lion. Suspicion and argument, contention, seem to be ingrained.

And this dissonance, this lack of harmony, is what makes lions such terrific challenges. Even the two apparently mellow ones here. And thus Roberta's dilemma: shall she take one of the docile cubs? Easier to train, simpler to "live" with over time. But then who will take the little gold hellion? What will become of her?

Roberta is not young, and she has mingled with wildlife nearly all of her life. Also, she has observed and even worked with a great many trainers. She reviews her long experience, as she weighs and balances the pros and cons of the choice she is about to make. Shall she take the easy way? Or shall she take on the challenge which she believes herself best fitted to handle among all the big-cat trainers she has ever known? Make the relatively lazy choice? Or choose the major and probably abiding challenge? Decide!

For hours on end, Roberta has watched the one bumptious cub push her sisters around, never allowing them to eat until she is physically restrained from the food bowl. And when the breeder *does* place the Alpha Lady away from the food, she runs over to take up a position at the water bowl on the opposite side of the enclosure.

And Roberta has watched that cub rise from the motionless pile of sleeping babies, then march back and forth on top of her two siblings, gnawing ears and tails and tender noses to get them awake to play because *she*, after all, is no longer sleepy. Roberta has seen the bully send a sister rolling, then sit on her stomach as a vantage point from which she attacks any part of that sister which dares to move. A tasseled tail that twitches unattended, she will chew until blood comes.

Now Roberta puts a hand on Billy's shoulder. "I've chosen. . . .Which one do you think?"

Billy's bright eyes pass over the little fiend to study the two appealing cubs. He shakes his head. Even after the hours of observation, he can hardly tell them apart. But his aunt is ready at long last.

"Speak up, kiddo. Which?"

Billy remains silent, his eyes on the mellow two. And yes, he is probably glad that the decision is not his to make.

"I've taken a lot of time," Roberta tells him softly, "because I needed to be sure." Now she gets the breeder's attention and points to the nasty one—the one with loads of confidence, a dauntless spirit and abundant *chutzpah*.

The man shakes his head. "It's true, she's a rascal," he mourns, not realizing that this one is her choice.

Billy, too, looks up with curiosity. "So which *do* you want, Auntie?"

"That one—that queen of the food bowl," Roberta tells him.

Billy's mouth falls open.

So does the breeder's. "No! You don't want her," he tells Roberta. "She'll be impossible to train. She's a devil."

"She's an angel!" Roberta insists. "Definitely my choice. Absolutely."

The man pulls back to stare at this animal trainer he has known and respected for twenty-five years. "Not a good joke," he says quietly. "You know I can't sell her—who'd want the little fiend?"

"*No* joke," Roberta insists. That is exactly what she'd thought. The difficult one would not easily find a home, might even be destroyed when she could not be placed.

"*I* want her! And her name will be *Malaika,* which is 'angel' in Swahili."

"Some *angel!*" the man snorts.

"Mala for short," the woman continues, "and you're invited to California a year from now . . . to admire our well-behaved lioness."

Then Roberta collects and signs the necessary papers, puts the burly lioness cub into a rugged carrier, and flies home with her favorite nephew and her prize cat.

Malaika was well trained in a year. That is, she moved to the back of her enclosure on (only) Roberta's command. And she stayed there obediently until food and water bowls were scrubbed and refilled and the flooring was cleaned. Like all wild creatures, though, and especially like all lions—she will never be tame. Now nine years later, she weighs over six hundred pounds and is still growing, still aggressive, still demanding—still a queen and certainly no angel. At the Foundation where she lives—sheltered, fed the right foods regularly, given medical attention as needed—she is likely to live more than twenty years. If she were in the wild, she could anticipate about fifteen maximum.

Mala is fierce in her love of "family" (pride) which includes Roberta and also those few volunteers at the wildlife foundation who pay her the regard she believes she deserves. One of her favorite people—besides herself, that is (she is convinced *absolutely* that she's a special member of the species *Homo sapiens)* is Larry, a local restaurateur who frequently brings extra raw meat to the Foundation. He insists on feeding Mala by hand—carefully, of course—through the mesh of her enclosure.

The huge lioness is still tough and mischievous. She's a spoiled brat, according to Roberta. Nephew Billy is now a strapping young man, and he considers Mala a barrel of laughs during the few (2-4) hours a day when she's not sleeping. (Lions are known as "the laziest animal in Africa.") Enhancement items (toys) in her enclosure must be rotated frequently or she becomes bored and "pacey." Volunteers who feed her have to be careful not to include fingers as appetizers.

And Mala retains that original personality and attitude. It is not easy for an adult lioness to hide herself in a thirty-foot-square enclosure having only a platform and one broad-entry den box lovely for sleeping on *top* of. But Mala manages to play hide-and-seek anyway. Can you imagine a ten-foot-long, three-foot-high creature crouching confidently behind a bowling ball? She manages this disguise in part by squinting so that she herself has a hard time seeing someone who comes up close.

A lioness who *squints?* Ah, not a lion but an angel. And if you ask Mala, she's just a regular citizen who helps to keep life interesting at Kirshner Wildlife Foundation.

18

The Cat Who Came
Out of the Cold

The family heard plaintive meows and followed the sound along the snowshoe trail in the late afternoon shadow of Mt. Lassen. They found the small furry creature at last, backed into a hollow among some redwood roots. He was distressed but full of fight and frenzy as the man removed his own jacket to roll into it the struggling bobcat cub.

"See that flat belly?" The three agreed that the cat was hungry, abandoned, too young to protect himself from predators and to find food in the sparse early spring. Without regard for stringent California laws about wildlife, the people decided to take home with them this *felis rufus* from the Sierras, to feed him up and tame him for a pet.

They named him Rufus and fed him cat kibble. He learned immediately where to find the food and water bowls, and he rapidly learned to use a litter box. But he hid or paced from window to door, hissing and spitting at the world in general, at people in particular, and slashing with needle claws at anyone pausing nearby. Six weeks passed with no improved attitude.

What did change was that Rufus got bigger and fiercer, able now to do real damage to furniture and drapes he clawed and to people who tried unsuccessfully to calm him.

Something had to be done. By using a broom, a shovel, and a leaf rake for a wild fifteen minutes, the family managed to herd the cat into the basement. They would feed and water him on the top landing, change his litter, and decide what to do next. By now, it was midsummer and hot even in the foothill town called Paradise, a couple thousand feet above Chico in the sweltering Sacramento Valley. Most homes left doors and windows open to capture any breeze, screens doing duty against insects.

Inevitably, someone who fed and watered Rufus left the basement door unlatched. And inevitably also, Rufus pressed against it, found himself free in the house. Going outside through a screen door was easy for a sixteen-pound animal. But he had no idea what to do outdoors; so entirely unobserved, he blasted through another screen to get into a neighboring house. There, he explored a little, sharpened his claws on the sofa back, then hunkered under the bed in the master bedroom to wait— presumably—for someone to feed him.

The drama played out on two stages. The family who brought Rufus from the mountains came home to an open basement door and torn screen. They knew it was useless to go out and call. But they were concerned that some child might get injured by finding and possibly cornering the animal, trying to treat him like an ordinary housecat. Except for the slim ear tufts and cheek ruffs—neither likely to be noticed by a young-ster—the animal looked like a *really big* grey-brown kitty with a rough, spotted coat and a bobbed white tail.

So knowing well that they would face legal action whether or not the cat was found, the family Rufus had been living with called the Department of Fish and Game. That the family took responsibility for the loose cat was what kept everyone out of jail, in the end. But the original rescuers didn't know that when they made the call.

Meantime, on the second stage, the neighbors came home late. They entered their bedroom—and were confronted by a large feline with fur fluffed as it sidled toward them, upper lip raised, growling, mouth open to hiss and spit. *Where was my dinner?*

They slammed the bedroom door as they rushed for the phone.

The original family was relieved to be rid of their surly pet. They cheerfully paid the hefty fine, grateful not to be sentenced in court. Rufus, meantime, was taken to a rehabilitation center. There, he was fed birds with the feathers on and rabbits complete with fur. He was not touched or spoken to, for he was to be returned to open forest in the mountains below Lassen.

The next step in the rehab process was to place live game into his enclosure. Would instinct take over? He had been abandoned so young that he had no experience with killing prey. But he came through that part of the program at the top of his class. What he did *not* do—what he *would* not do!—was eat what he caught.

"Wait'll he's hungry—then he'll feed fast enough," predicted one official.

But Rufus continued to kill whatever went to him—always prey he was likely to find in the wild—and then ignore it. He grew slim and finally thin. The Center started over, once more giving him fresh-killed prey. This he ate with gusto, soon regaining his former weight. But when live prey was re-introduced, history repeated. He caught and killed expertly, but would not eat it.

"Guess he refuses to fix his own meals," one official mourned.

"We can't release him up there to starve," said another.

"Well, he sure can't live here for the rest of his life." A thirty-year-old bobcat is not unusual in captivity.

After two more attempts to start him with dead prey and move him to live—both with the same result—everyone agreed that putting him down was the only logical answer. Euthanasia. But for a healthy, year-old bobcat? Might some other solution be possible?

And then by means of an invisible network that mysteriously links wildlife trainers and breeders and conservators all over the world, Kirshner Wildlife heard about Rufus. Roberta Kirshner called the Rehab Center and offered to take him.

Fish and Game hated to put down a robust animal. But Rufus was not your ordinary bobcat, and they explained this fact on the phone. "You'll never train him. He's one stubborn cat."

"Maybe I can't," Roberta said—never believing for one moment that this was the case. That stubborn cat was going to be a challenge, that's all. She could hardly wait. "But I'll take care of him in any case—give him a good quality of life here at the shelter," she promised. Then, assuming that silence on the line was agreement, "Can you drop him off?"

The bobcat named Rufus has been at Kirshner's for three years at this writing. From the beginning, he seemed comfortable in the cyclone-fenced, fifteen-foot cube where he was placed with toys and a cozy den-box on a wooden platform. A split-level abode, why not? He has no trouble eating the raw red meat and chicken supplied to him—six pounds divided among four meals a day. But then, he never did have any problem with eating what someone else prepared.

What's changed totally, though, is his outlook. Roberta not only trained him to respect and obey her, but she also taught him how to behave like a civilized cat. He's a young adult weighing in at twenty-three pounds . . . and still growing.

"You can't ever tame a wild creature," Roberta insists to anyone who asks, "but you can *train* almost any healthy animal." Even Rufus—if the trainer is patient enough, persistent enough, and sufficiently knowledgeable. "But never confuse 'trained' with 'tamed,'" she tells the six Kirshner assistants whom Rufus allows in his enclosure.

In a 2003 issue of *I Love Cats* was a picture of Rufus standing on the lap of teenager and future veterinarian Dallas Wentz. She's one of the six. When she or any of the others goes in, that person sits on the edge of the platform and talks. Rufus comes out of his den box and jumps up onto the roof of the wooden cube. He purrs. The visitor continues with mild speech, using his name a lot. Now the cat puts his soft paws down onto the person's head. He gently rearranges the hair. If it was up, he loosens it. If it was loose, he knots it up.

"In another life, he was 'Mr. Rufus,' a highly successful coiffurist," quips one of the chosen six.

Next the sturdy cat jumps down onto the platform and pads up onto the lap. From there, still standing, he rubs his head under that person's chin to elicit stroking. His purrs can be heard ten feet away, beyond the outer fence. Resembling a giant-sized domestic, he circles several times before lowering himself to snuggle onto the friendly lap. The volunteer pets him. With each caress, the cat pushes against the hand . . . until he falls asleep.

"Remember, you can train 'em but never really *tame* them," Roberta asserts about the wildlife with which she has worked for almost five decades. Concerning Rufus, she only shakes her head. "He's just different, I guess."

19

Beware The Fisher Cat!

I am standing in my pajamas on the carpet beside the bed. Every hair on my arms is erect, also those at the back of my neck. My eyes focus on the wall clock showing 3:15—yes, A.M.—in dim light. But every other sense is fastened on the screams which seem to come from just outside my bedroom window. Varied with shrieks, yowls, moans, screeches . . . sustained, continuing, endless. Intensity only increases. Pain, suffering—anguish, wrenching sobs. I glance over to the other side of the bed. Doug lies there peacefully, undisturbed. Lucky him.

The horror occurring outside does not slacken. Someone is being attacked—a young woman? Moans, howls—sustained and apparently endless. The shrieks are female-sounding, and she needs help. Agony, wrenching sobs.

I slide into my slippers. I will have to intervene—go outside armed with . . . what? Our very largest flashlight? I am halfway to the bedroom door when the sound ceases. No winding down, no hiccups or sighs or whimpers, only silence. Has someone been murdered?

I am now shivering all over—perhaps anxiety, probably cold, but certainly on edge, adrenaline still rushing, muscles alert, ready for fight or flight. Calm yourself!

We live in woodlands, a fair distance from neighbors. And no sound remains—only stillness beyond my still-ringing ears. It is inky out there, and as a newcomer to New Hampshire, I have no idea what I'd be dealing with if I went into the moonless black out there brightened only by this puny flashlight. Going into that bleak silence . . . where is it that *bravery* becomes *foolhardiness?* All right, I'm a coward.

But what could make those terrible noises? How long were the sounds going on before I awakened and leapt from bed? And then how lengthily sustained for hour-long minutes while I stood here . . . ? Perhaps I experienced a nightmare—I, who never have recollection of any dream. I glance again at the bed. Doug still lies there, breathing regularly, unperturbed. A fantasy, then, my private illusion?

I've been living here in New England, east of the Mississippi and very far east of home in Northern California— for how long? Two months? Yes, I'm a stranger in a strange land, but nothing in my prior experience approaches what I've just now heard. Not the roaring of a lion close by. Not the trumpet of a bull elephant annoyed. . . .

The next morning, I describe for Doug my auditory encounter of the night.

He nods. "You know, I think I may have heard that sound a time or two."

I stare at him. He's lived here forty-some years. But he does sleep soundly. "And?"

He shrugs. "May have been a fisher. Furry critter of some kind. I've never seen one, that I know of, but I've heard about them. They're capable of kicking up quite a fuss."

A *fuss*??? Doug tends to understate.

At eleven that morning, I motor the three or so miles down our winding, tree-lined highway into town and enter the coffee shop, my source of iced tea, local people and current information.

Dispassionately as possible, I describe the sounds I heard last night.

"Fisher cat!" several people say at once.

I look around, see frowns and wrinkled up noses, bared teeth . . . general displeasure.

"What's a fisher cat?" I wonder aloud.

Ginny owns the shop and answers first. "Animal—wild animal, not a cat at all, biggish weasel. And I doubt that they ever go fishing."

Someone named Jacqueline chimes in. "Horrible animals. They've killed every cat I've ever had."

General agreement among patrons.

"They usually don't even eat everything they kill!" comments a man I've never seen before.

Another five heads nod agreement.

"Cats? Just pull them apart and spread them out on the ground."

More nodding. "And chickens!" Noses are still wrinkled, and frowns still mark features. "They'll wipe out a henhouse, eat maybe two fowl."

After that, people talk among each other about "fishers they have known" and I hear repeats on cat slayings and chicken-yard invasions.

Are these people putting me on? They know I'm new here. What they don't know is that I'm quite knowledgeable about animals, especially wildlife. I've studied and reported on it, published articles on the subject for years, visited and observed it in the U.S., throughout much of Asia and parts of Africa.

So why haven't I ever heard of a "fisher cat" before? Fish*ing* cat, yes. In Southeast Asia. The smallish, jungle cat with a flattish head that actually waits and watches the water until it can swipe out a fish for its meal. Or will even splash in after it! Fierce if threatened, yes; but otherwise mellow with a recognizably feline voice.

"Fisher cat? You're sure?" I ask those around me. They nod soberly, faces still registering distaste. I finish my iced tea and leave.

At home in my office, I get on line before venturing between the covers of books. Yep, something called a "fisher" exists! The appellation "fisher *cat*" appears to be used chiefly in New England. Long and lean and agile like the common marten and mink; short legged, fast and furry, the fisher too is a mustelid (a weasel)—but larger than the relatives named, and further identified as "the largest of the martens." A full-grown adult male can weigh as much as eighteen pounds (record weight is twenty) and can be as much as three feet long—*plus* more than a full foot of bushy tail.

The coat is often dark and thick, may lighten and thin in different seasons, often with a hoariness on chest and head. Wearing these thick coats, fishers easily adapt to the cold winds and snow of rigorous winters and high altitudes. Still relatively common in Canada and Alaska, fishers have inhabited (and in some regions still do inhabit) the most isolated northern tier of the "lower forty-eight" states, plus high country of Appalachia and even the southern High Sierras.

According to Fish and Wildlife, fishers have been seriously decimated and in many locales wiped out through over hunting to acquire the rich (and once-valuable) pelt.

The fisher is both terrestrial and arboreal. A hollow portion of tree—watch out, squirrels!—is a favored lodging and is almost always the nest for newborns. But this animal will dig temporary quarters in the ground or even a snowdrift if necessary. Whatever lodging is selected, though, must be among trees, preferably woodlands of predominantly evergreen. And at least in the past, a place generally isolated (unpeopled).

And the fisher is versatile. A large part of its adaptability relates to the unusual feet. Like wolverines, all four are extra large, wider than they are long, the fisher having unsheathed but retractable claws, thus able to function as snowshoes. Because of especially flexible ankle joints, those feet can rotate almost 180 degrees. This ability allows a fisher to descend a tree trunk headfirst—something our domestic cats *wish* they could do! A round patch of hair located on the central pad of each back foot marks plantar glands which emit a distinctive odor probably related to territory marking and other possible communication. That these patches enlarge during mating season suggests that the emission also relates to reproduction.

A private and for the most part solitary animal by *strong* preference, fishers are largely but not exclusively nocturnal, can be crepuscular. The male in particular "gets around." He claims a territory of 50 to 150 square miles, and this range can be enlarged in a tough winter, much diminished in a time of plenty. Although the female "marks" a smaller territory, both males and females insist—except for the brief mating season—on living their lives well away from even their own kind.

The female fisher is smaller and has a finer, softer pelt. I have found no evidence, however, to suggest that she has a "kinder, gentler" nature. The reproductive cycle for fishers is about one year because the female employs delayed implantation. Mating time is late March to early April. But the blastocyst doesn't attach until around the middle of February that next year. In about fifty days of active gestation, one to six kits are born. . . . and the female enters estrus about a week later.

Born helpless, siblings still in the "nest" start squabbling with each other seriously soon after three months, sometimes injuring or even killing one another before their mother turns them out at around four months. From that moment, the juvenile is forever on his or her own for survival.

Return of the Fisher

A news item mailed to me and taken from the Chico (CA) *Enterprise-Record* in early 2011 recounts how an animal "long and sadly missing from this territory" is now being re-introduced in the northern Sierra foothills and mountains. . . . Ah yes, the fisher!

And from the southern Sierras, where fishers still survive, the San Diego *Union Tribune* (Katie Zezima) announced ". . . Fishers Rebound: Backyard Pets Become Prey."

Dr. Lori Gibson of Rhode Island's Fish and Wildlife Division says that the state got forty-three complaints about fishers in 2009 alone—largely regarding attacks on pets.

So . . . It may be misleading to describe these animals being released as some kind of cuddly pussycat.

Fishers are one of the few animals known to prey on porcupines. Most predators steer clear of *Erithizon dorsatum* because these stickery creatures have sharp quills and know how to use them. But fishers bite repeatedly at the unquilled face until the porcupine is completely dazed, badly injured or dead. Then the fisher flips the animal over to feast from the (also un-quilled) stomach.

A porcupine, however, can be a fierce adversary. Sometimes the fisher "loses," may even be mortally wounded. Witnesses to a fisher/porcupine confrontation say that the clash may last for half an hour or more.

Although the fisher is a capable swimmer, the creature appears to show no partiality for fish but *is* known to eat about anything, not only meat and in tough times carrion and even vegetables and fruit, certainly seeds. Its preferences, though, run to not only (and especially) porcupines but also squir-rels and chipmunks, rabbits including snowshoe hares, even mice—whatever is equal or smaller in size and can be outrun, out-wrestled and overcome. Certainly chickens. Small dogs. And yes, they seem to have a "thing" (although apparently no particular hunger) for domestic cats.

A fisher certainly does not meow, so where does the feline appellation come from? One theory which has some credibility (at least logic) is that the animal was originally noted by Dutch immigrants in New England and, as the proclivities of the an-imal became known, got dubbed *"fizzor"* or (variant) *"visse,"* both being Netherlander terms for "nasty." Another explana-tion, this one attributed to Old English and to current French, is that the word for a polecat (various weasels) is *fiche* or *fichet.*

And what about the "cat" which is attached to the name in New England? A fisher certainly does not "meow," so where does New England's feline appellation come from? The jury's still out on this one.

One must remember that fishers may be blamed unjustly

for harming domestic animals taken by other predators such as coyotes, bobcats, dog packs and even bears and mountain lions. Okay, and probably. But what I heard that memorable night was none of these "other predators" named (I know their sounds) . . . and that creature sounded capable of taking just about anything—possibly by decibels alone.

20

Piles and Piles of Crocodiles

"Stop scratching and watch the water," Virote growls at the boy sitting behind him in the dugout. "You should be wearing long sleeves, long pants. I *warned you!*"

"*Rawn mag,*" Uthai answers softly. Too hot. The youngster brushes a mosquito from his forehead, then scratches with both hands at the bites festering above his left knee. His brain is working with the same vigor, as it has for the three days and nights he and Virote have been in the steamy swamp. Uthai has come here to learn. To make an important decision. He is after all twelve years old, and he lives in Siam, a magic place where in 1939 all things are possible.

And yes! He *will* return to his home in Bangkok and there—yes!—turn his own yard into a wetland. He grins in the darkness as he scans the water all around.

And then—"LOOK!" He rises dangerously high in the tiny craft to point out two glowing red embers lit by Virote's torch in the inky marsh. "Maybe a big one." Those bright glints of reptile eyes are well spaced.

"Watch out!" Virote straightens up smoothly to a kneeling position and takes aim with his crossbow.

Uthai hears the *"twang-ng-ng"* from release of the metal-tipped bolt. He winces as twisted rope from a coil behind him sears his shoulder when it sizzles past.

The hollowed-out log in which the two crouch suddenly tilts. It swerves toward shore, then bounces back into the channel. Uthai rolls up dripping line as he rapidly brings it aboard. Then he sits on the pile. No bit of rope should fall into the water. There, it could snare the crocodile as it passes beneath their boat—and overturn the dugout and its occupants. The boy braces himself in the plunging craft as the desperate reptile dives to escape the iron shaft in its brain.

Three nights of hunting have bagged only this one three-meter crocodile which is worth sixty baht—three U.S. dollars—on the Bangkok market. Uthai's friend Virote is a professional croc hunter who can no longer make a living from collecting crocodiles. Too few remain.

"Here's the biggest I've seen in three years," he says as they tie the carcass to the stern hook. Then he laughs. "And here *you* are, learning to cure hides—a worthless trade now in 1939!"

"But the market for leather is strong," Uthai says. "People pay huge prices for croc hide made up into belts, wallets, shoes, purses—beautiful, durable leather."

"Five years at most," Virote declares, "and you won't find a decent-sized croc in all of Siam!"

Uthai knows the truth in what his friend says. In fact, the boy is making this trip *because* the reptiles are so scarce. He begged to come because he wanted to see where and how crocodiles live in the wild. And the excursion has been worthwhile—even with the heat and humidity, the bad drinking water, the hordes of crawling, biting, stinging insects. He has gained valuable information. He now knows that a young croc likes shallow, warm water away from adult male crocodiles—exactly what Uthai can supply at his family home in Bangkok.

This knowledge is a start. For Uthai has had responsibilities since his father died a year ago. He must support his mother, younger brother and two sisters. He has left school and apprenticed himself to a tanner, a sad ancient man who pays Uthai by allowing him to keep his tips for delivering cured hides ordered by leather workers around Bangkok. The boy has little formal education. And after purchase of minimal groceries each week, he has no money at all.

But he does have a dream. It is a long-held fantasy which has become tangible during these uncomfortable nights of floating on black marsh that mirrors their torchlight. And never until this one time, he reminds himself with secret satisfaction, has the dark water reflected the crimson eyes of a crocodile.

"I'm going to raise crocodiles for a business," he announces to Virote the next morning.

"You're . . . *bah!*" Crazy.

Uthai shrugs. "I'll get hatchlings fairly fresh from the egg. We've seen plenty of those. I'll keep them safe, feed them, and they'll grow. Then I'll use their handsome hides to fashion shoes and handbags—whatever rich people want." His dark eyes dance. "I'll make lots of money!"

Virote roars with laughter. "What do you know about raising crocodiles? What does *any*one know?"

"Nothing, but you'll teach me."

"*Me!* I can find them if there are some to be found—which there aren't, not anymore. I can shoot them, skin them, get the hides to Bangkok. But *raise* them?" He chuckles. "I know nothing."

"What do they eat?"

". . . Fish, I guess. Animals . . . each other."

"Each other!" Dismay.

"Bulls eat the babies when they can—probably why the little nippers hang around in puddles for a year or two."

"But you could bring me those young crocs?"

Virote shakes his head slowly. "Tell me you're not serious about this."

"*Live* young ones."

". . . I guess. Those we see plenty of, you're right. But it takes years and years to grow a crocodile."

It took more than years, as Uthai discovered. Raising crocs took hard work, many supplies . . . and endless patience. No one he knew of had ever tried to farm crocodiles before. No one could give him advice, and no instruction manual existed. The youngster built on his dream gradually through trial and a great deal of error.

In long hours beyond those required for his tanning apprenticeship, the growing boy dug shallow pits in his back yard, filled them with water, and turned loose live crocodile babies brought him by Virote and a few other hunter friends. The small creatures died. More were brought, and they also died.

Uthai learned that a foot-long baby croc is more delicate than a human baby—and far less lovable. They bite the hand that feeds them, along with the toes and ankles of that benefactor.

They are always hungry; but a fishbone can be lethal; also a piece of string or wood or wire. At nearby rivers and khlongs, those endless canals of Bangkok, Uthai patiently whirled out his circular net to seine water creatures. But he learned that the snappish reptiles will die from overeating, too—even their natural fare of fish.

Everything could be fatal for these small crocs. Flies and mosquitoes could cause blindness. Nearby loud sounds including thunder terrified them—they could go into shock and drown. Rarely a problem in this tropical land, but water too chilly (below 48° F.) caused paralysis also. The animals were unable to breathe, so suffocated.

Because no reptile is able to perspire, even a grown crocodile will literally bake in hot sun if unable to reach cool water or deep shade.

Uthai's mother confronted him. "If this is a good business, why does no one else do it?"

"It's hard work," Uthai told her. "And it's experimental—who can tell what will happen?"

His mother folded her arms and set her lips tightly. "A *bad* business."

"But no one else has thought of it!"

"That makes it good?"

Uthai nodded happily. "No competition."

By 1950, Uthai had on his back doorstep a hundred adolescent crocodiles—and in his ears, many neighbor complaints. His large yard could no longer contain the reptiles' growth, their fierce competition for food, the odor of their unhealthy crowding. And the young man was learning that—even with same-size animals—too many crocs in too small space turn cannibal.

By this time, wild crocodiles were all but extinct in the kingdom, and the value of good skins had skyrocketed. So although Uthai hated reducing his stock, he chose only three strong breeding pairs to save. Releasing the smallest ones into river wetlands, he sold off all the crocodiles large enough to have hide with commercial value.

Oldest Living Crocodile in Captivity Makes Guinness Book of World Records

The Crocodile Farm's Chai Yai [Mister Big] celebrated his 33rd birthday on 10 June 2010. He is 19' 8" long and weighs 1¼ tons. In croc years, though, Chai Yai is a mere adolescent. Receiving good food and medical attention, this crocodile is much larger and probably much more healthy than he would be in the wild.

Now with a little cash for expansion, he spent a small amount for one rai (1/5 acre) of swampy land just east of Bangkok near the town of Samut Prakarn. He chose well, for the property was surrounded by similar undeveloped rai lowland and flood plain that he would later purchase.

His uncle tried to counsel him. "Rabbits grow up in two months. People eat the meat and sell the fur. No family raising rabbits can go hungry."

Uthai nodded respectfully, then replied, "And rabbits are small, plentiful and cheap." He sometimes fed rabbits to his crocodiles, but he didn't admit that to his uncle.

"So instead, you choose something ugly and unfriendly that requires *six years* to have value! And who would eat crocodile flesh?" The man spat in contempt.

But no one could change Uthai's mind as he gained confidence and skill. He knew where he was going. By 1960 when he was thirty-five, he was called "Khun Uthai"—*Mister* Uthai— with respect, for he owned three thousand healthy crocodiles plus a thriving business in beautifully crafted hide.

And every year, he carefully selected at first one and then several pairs of healthy, fully-grown crocs to release in one or another swamp throughout the kingdom now called "Thailand" instead of "Siam."

When—as a measure to protect this endangered species—North America placed a ban on the import and sale of crocodile products, those items certified as coming from Khun Uthai's Crocodile Farm were exempt from the prohibition. This far-thinking man could and did prove that success for his Farm meant a gradual replenishment of crocs in the wild.

In 1980, when the Crocodile Farm had thirty thousand saurians on 150 rai of land, Khun Uthai was chosen Thailand's Businessman of the Year. And although no longer a youngster, his original enthusiasm remained as his youthful dream continued to be realized and expanded.

Another part of Khun Uthai's dream, though, exists hundreds of kilometers away from his Crocodile Farm. . . . Those breeding, healthy pairs from long ago and the still-continuing release are free to roam in marshy sloughs throughout the country. Because no more crocodile hunters exist in Thailand, the reptiles have a far better chance at survival than did their ancestors.

A pleasant thought in these days of vanishing species, that Thai crocodiles are somewhere in some oozing waterway once more, vigorous and multiplying slowly . . . always very slowly.

This story is based loosely on some bilingual interviews in 1981—both of us endeavoring to speak (with spotty success) in the other's language—with Khun Uthai Youngprapakorn of the Crocodile Farm and Zoo at Samut Prakarn near Bangkok in Thailand.

"I'm still building my dream," he said then of his rapidly expanding business—an operation that by 2012 included (by report) more than 200,000 reptiles. Two of his sons are veterinary doctors and a daughter has long had her master's degree in Business Administration. The Youngprapakorn family includes grandchildren and great-grandchildren, most being educated and trained to be a part of their Crocodile Farm—now the largest establishment of its kind in the world.

One daughter, Patcharapimol, has recently branched off from the family enterprise to build a separate farm source to produce from not only crocodilians but also other exotic materials (snakes, etc.) high-end wallets, purses and bags for international trade. She envisions outlets in Singapore, Hongkong and even France.

More Thais than tourists come daily to view Asian wildlife in near-natural surroundings. Tigers, clouded leopards, elephants, gibbons, pythons, a variety of civets and one grouchy gaur, that huge, rare bovine—to name a few. Sorted by size for their own safety, occupying eight huge ponds in addition to the many nursery areas for hatchlings and juveniles, crocodiles are what flood the Farm population and today float grizzled and sleepy (except at mealtime) as they grow . . . *grow* . . . **grow**. . . .

At this writing (2012), Khun Uthai is 87 years old.

* Note: when I lived in Thailand in the '70's and '80's, the sizable wildlife collection at the Crocodile Farm had by far the healthiest, cleanest and most content animals in captivity of any I ever saw elsewhere in the Kingdom, including and especially any zoo.

21

(Keeping It Off)

The High Cost of Corpulence

Don't read this, please, if you're not a weight warrior—it'll disgust you. You don't want fat to be a way of life. You *think* thin. But certain words mean pain that cannot ever be fathomed by the trim, the slim, the petite. *Obese . . . fleshy . . . plump . . . chubby . . . stout . . .* I still hate those words.

And while *avoirdupois* is a system of weights to some, and therefore unloaded as a noun, fat folks consider the term a potential adjective. They see the world around them through an avoirdupoigenous blur. Because fat people aren't "worthy." That's how our western world looks at overweight people; and therefore that's how overweight people learn to look at themselves. Especially overweight women.

Security decreases in direct proportion to the amount of excess poundage. If ponderous Polly aches, she *deserves* to ache—look at that ballast. And she mustn't become tired— what can she expect, lugging that lard? And she must not ever be hungry—good lord, she could survive for a year on stored flesh! Never mind that a fat person is the hungriest human around—for food, yes; but also for social acceptance, for self respect and especially for confidence.

Hungry! It's terrifying to be a third class citizen.

So we do something about it. We torture our bodies into lankiness and emerge somewhat dazed but triumphant between fat periods, holding our breath because we recognize this bit of slim as temporary. It's only a matter of time before we relax and start munching our individual ways toward heft.

Sure, we can lose weight if we want to badly enough. But *keeping it off*—there's the proverbial rub! I know. I've lost seventeen hundred and thirty pounds since I reached puberty. And I'm a lucky one: I've never been "obese," only *heavy.* Let me tell you about it.

Throughout the time I was growing up and ever outward, three refrains echoed in my youthful ears.

"WHAT A FINE, HEALTHY GIRL!" exclaimed the friends of my mother. And always said with approval. I learned eventually that I'd arrived in an undernourished, four-pound condition at birth, a risky situation in the early 1930's. Thus, Mother's friends were delighted and amazed to see husky, hefty, dimpled little me. . . .

In third grade, I weighed a gargantuan seventy-two pounds, the tallest and heaviest kid in my grade. Much exclamation . . . much pride on my part. I got a gold star on my health card and an announcement in front of the room by the approving white-frocked school nurse. Not one contender in my class existed during those Depression days when few people ate regularly or much.

Somehow, we always managed to have food on our table throughout that dreary decade in the Midwest while I established eating habits. Not salad or vegetables except during spring and summer months when the garden was producing—but plenty of potatoes boiled, baked, mashed and scalloped. My father's preference was "fried." We had home made bread. And at every meal, some kind of meat complete with rich brown gravy from the drippings.

Plus, my mother and grandmother (who lived with us) could bake magnificent pies! But the fact is, people didn't know or even care much about nutrition, in those days of the 30's and even 40's, when I was growing up. The object was to *have* food—any kind of food there during the Depression and later of certain foods (sugar, meat, canned goods) in the rationing of World War II.

I should elaborate on the family about body weight. My mother was extremely large, well over three hundred pounds (I peeked once and saw a 360 on her special scale); but she was energetic, active, committed to teaching fifth graders. She was always ready to hike with me through Fontenelle Forest in bluffs just south of the city. She organized week end fishing and camping trips along the Missouri River, was a main mover and shaker for a two-weeks-long church camp in western Nebraska every summer. Despite size—and she had to purchase all attire except shoes by mail from Lane Bryant—she was an active woman deeply involved with church and community.

The maternal grandmother—who lived with us—was determined to feed (*stuff!*) everyone around her. Her oft-voiced mantra: "Eat a bite of bread-and-butter between every forkful of your meal." An irony of nature, she was svelte, never weighing an extra ounce (as I recall her). But her children were *large,* as in grossly overweight. Her husband, the grandfather I never knew, died from diabetes before I was born, as did her elder son while still a young adult. My mother was eldest and tallest, actually quite beautiful except for the extra flesh. Her next-youngest sister was "petite." That term in the clothing business, as has been explained to me, refers to *height,* not *girth,*. "Petite" sizes run the usual gamut from a diminutive 3 or 4 or possibly less right up to an elephantine 28 or 30 or possibly more. But that aunt, although short, made my own mother seem positively Lilliputian. The third and youngest sister *had been* enormous.

"She ate almost nothing, just drank tea for years," my mother reported to me when I was grown. "And she ruined her health when she made herself thin."

Just a note: the middle sister died of asthma at age thirty-six; my own mother died at age sixty-five after insertion of a pacemaker following a heart attack; and the youngest sister who had "ruined her health" (and who, by the way, smoked until the day she died) succumbed to bone cancer at age eighty.

My father was not particularly large, nor was anyone on his side of the family; and he was the one bringing those big Russian and German genes to bear. I was my parents' only child—and at that a tardy decision, if indeed having a child *was* an actual decision in those days—Mother being thirty-five when I was born. From her family came British, Norwegian and American Indian chromosomes. And sturdy stuff is in there somewhere!

Despite impact contributed by heredity, however (an ever handy copout), my weight was surely connected to food consumption.

And it was still during those elementary school years that the second verse with the same unvoiced chorus reached my ears—and always in third person, when someone is eleven years old: "SHE CERTAINLY IS LARGE FOR HER AGE."

Well, I was! And what had been a source of hauteur in the third grade . . . wasn't, anymore. For one thing, I was savvy enough to know that people who remarked on this ratio of size to age rarely knew how old I *was.* Nor did they ask, neither before nor after their comment. It was safe to surmise, therefore, that I was a big girl for *any* age. Oh, indeed.

In the teenage years when fat was frantic and big was anything *but* beautiful, I got the third verse of the same song: "MY, HOW YOU'VE GROWN!" Never mind that the speaker had seen me only last Saturday. Migawd, I was still growing . . . by the minute, with every breath I took!

I tried to console myself that this person probably had a very bad memory. But I thought about the statement while I chewed my dinner. And again while I devoured my late evening snack, watching teensy Dorothy Collins with trim Snooky Lansen on *Hit Parade*. I remember brooding on the subject while I consumed three tall glasses of ice cold milk during the wrestling matches that followed.

Exercise wasn't a factor—I was a long-time member of a performing acrobatic dance troupe. Was first baseman on a women's softball team that practiced after classes on most afternoons of the school week and daily during school breaks. Had vigorous domestic duties which included the household laundry and the care and cleaning for the upstairs rooms that my mother rented out.

It was necessary to stop growing. Food consumption had to be the key. Grandma was long gone, by then, along with her feeding compulsion. My father with his affinity for fried potatoes had died of the 'flu' when I was nine. Mother and I ate whatever was available and quick after her long day at work. Meat, inevitably bread with butter, and salad or some kind of vegetable. A quickie favorite in the household was hamburger gravy over toast with (or without) sliced tomatoes on the side.

We never talked about poundage, Mother and I. No doubt, each thought our private thoughts on the unpopular subject.

During those adolescent days, I'd pick at the food before me, often passing up green beans to afford a second pork chop. I'd forego the breakfast egg so that I could have a second slice of toast liberally buttered and jellied. And then . . . when one goes without lunch at school, it's all right to have a ten-cent root beer float at the soda fountain after school on the way to the bus stop. Isn't it?

But then I'd get so depressed when after a week of such starvation I'd not lost a single pound that I'd purchase a dozen *kolachés* at the Bohemian bakery near our house and devour every one of these fruit-filled pastries.

My secret *Conceal-and-Gulp* theory was uncollapsed for years: what one eats in private doesn't count. I remember a limerick my grandmother could chant. I don't know that she said it for me, but I've never forgotten the words:

There was a young lady named Liz
Whose figure was mostly a fizz.
She never was able
To eat at the table,
But in the back pantry—gee whiz!

Just as Grandma was loaded with pithy limericks, I was full of hypotheses—based usually on hope rather than logic. How about this one?

If you eat fast, you won't get fat . . .

But the rational truth dawned tardily:

If you eat fast, you can consume twice the amount in half the time.

I read a medical statement several years back to the effect that it takes fifteen minutes for appetite to wear off regardless of how much or how little one eats. Imagine how much food can be bolted down by an accomplished fast eater (me) during the quarter-hour wait. Consumption is limited only by the food supply.

My beginning, then: not fat yet, only "impending" weight—certainly not svelte, but healthy and hearty and active and growing. . . . Cheer leader. Captain of the softball team. Camp counselor and instructor for archery and tennis. Barrel racing when the rodeo was around. Enough social life to stay afloat, but not so much that I couldn't stay abreast (so to speak) on Saturday nights of _Hit Parade_ and _TV Wrestling_. And of course chomping away to bigger dimensions right along. I knew and my wardrobe knew that I was—horrors!—still burgeoning.

For a while in my adult life, I let myself fall for that "big bones" nonsense proffered by friends who liked me anyway. But my bones would soon have to be the size of _tyrannosaurus rex_ to justify the poundage, and they aren't. Math isn't a strong suit for me, but I once figured that I'd be nicely proportioned (good and skinny!) at a height of seven feet, three inches. Lacking pituitary problems, there existed but one alternative: lose weight.

I spoke of weight problems to three different doctors during my rare sorties into the medical world—two babies and a particularly severe tonsillitis were my total exposures after infancy until age twenty-five. (Healthy, remember?) All three physicians had always been slim and always would be. Therefore, all three considered themselves authorities on the subject of weight loss.

"So simple," they said, "just eat less."

I've known people who get up one morning and murmur, "Oh-oh! This dress is too snug. Gotta drop some pounds." And then they do it. The clothes in their wardrobes range from sizes 8 to 10, the eights running large while the tens are sized a bit small.

I am not one of these people. Neither are you, if you're still reading this. I've said on at least a hundred mornings of my life, "Gotta drop some pounds. I'll start next Monday." With anticipated righteousness, then, I've stuffed my face for the rest of the week. And when Monday actually arrived, I may or may not have started dieting. What I did hardly mattered; for late or soon the result would be the same: *fat*. The clothing in my wardrobe ranged from size 12 to 22. The 12's may have run large, but those 22's were not sized small. And I've worn them all, temporarily, again and again.

It's no surprise that a fat person is hypersensitive. Certain words in the most ordinary vocabulary make the person cringe. Innocuous words like *chew* and *grow* and even *look*. Innocent little questions and observations can turn someone like me into a pulsating blob of agony.

"Wouldn't you like another carrot stick?"

No, I'd rather have a third helping of tapioca pudding, dammit!

"Whatever became of that beautiful green blouse I like so much?"

I outgrew it along with everything else in my wardrobe, dammit.

"But I thought you enjoyed slalom skiing."

I do, but there's not an outboard on the lake that can get me out of the water on one ski, dammit.

When someone sees herself as "fat," she tries harder, like Avis. She studies hard and bats hard and sings hard and works hard and house cleans hard. She develops her intellect and her muscles and her senses of humor, perception, rhythm, design, balance, coordination and fairness. She develops everything except her physical self. That, she ignores and hopes that everyone else will do the same. She tries to forget. . . . After all, she didn't select this particular body model, did she?

And she watches her slender friends gorge themselves without gaining the proverbial ounce. She sits around feeling sorry for herself. She wishes that mirrors had never been created, that eyesight were not humankind's primary means for sensing the environment. She becomes analytical and philosophical and deals in the subjunctive mood: "If Moses had seen me, there'd be another commandment!"

Understand, I'm not looking for sympathy. Nor for scorn and disgust. You see, I've never been wobble-jowled, low-energy, shake-and-shiver enormous. Just big. And physicians don't get excited about *big,* only *obese.* Like the man with a cold encouraged to develop pneumonia so that he can be cured.

"Is there anything," I once asked my doctor, "that I can eat absolutely all I want of?"

"Certainly," he grinned. "Lettuce."

So I loaded up the refrigerator, munched and crunched and lunched all week end on lettuce alone. Delicious! Innocent! By Monday, I'd gained two pounds.

The first serious diet was in 1955, more than fifty years ago. At the absolute, all-time *most* I've ever weighed before or since, some sixty pounds beyond all former or subsequent pinnacles, I went to a physician who had lost his own eyesight from diabetes.

"He *cares* about overweight," the recommending friend promised me, "because he cares a great deal about diabetes."

And he did! He diagnosed me slightly hypothyroid and borderline diabetic, and gave me prescriptions for both thyroxin and—to help along my weight loss and frame of mind—Methedrine. This latter was legal in those halcyon days.

And thus I, who had consumed never more than three aspirins per year in my previous existence, began religiously to pop pills. Eating less was not difficult, suddenly. . . . I really didn't have time for such a sedentary activity. I was up day and night—doing, doing, doing. . . . My having at the time a very full time job and first one, then two babies at home still in diapers, this new bluster of energy and my certainty of well-being all worked out handily.

And I lost weight: sixty-six pounds in six months. Slim and trim and quite pleased with the world and me in it. Friends were begging me to "put some weight on, Phyl! You're skin and bones!" These entreaties let me know that I was "beginning to get there." Wasn't it Wallis Simpson, the Duchess of Windsor, who observed that no woman can ever be too rich or too thin?

Sometimes, I missed being able to sleep; but mostly, the whole new syndrome was just fine. Even with my weight finally acceptable, I was afraid to stop the pills—although contrary to current beliefs, I never did need or want to increase the dosage.

Several attenuated years passed. Then two things happened. People in authority legislated felony status to people like me who took even prescriptive methodrine for dieting. And my blind, understanding doctor died. In six months of being surrounded by delectable foodstuffs—and all foodstuffs can be delectable if one has the appropriate attitude—I once again woke up morning after morning with the knowledge that I *must* lose weight.

"Are you unhappy?" a doctor asked me.

"Only about being fat," said I.

"Are you under tension?" he probed.

"Yes, about *being fat.*" I wasn't trying to be difficult. But when I'm happy, I eat. Sad? More food. Tense? The same. For me, eating is a symptom of being alive.

Now came the starvation diets. They did fine up to the minute when I ceased to starve.

"Your stomach is certainly shrunk," I told myself sternly. "You won't be *able* to eat much."

Not true. Within twenty-four hours my stomach was back to its normal rapacious capacity and urging, "More, more!"

Why can't I have a *nervous* stomach? Why won't it rebel at strange combinations? I know several people who like cold pizza for breakfast. And I know one person who likes bacon on jelly toast *any* time. I know some ice cream freaks, some having switched over to frozen yogurt by now. But *I'm* the only person I know who cherishes all of the above . . . and more!

The high-protein diet meant eggs and meat and lots of water. That was good for a quick thirty-seven pounds plus a monumental case of halitosis. And when I stopped, forty-one pounds returned almost magically. Ah, weight! Removed with such difficulty and restored so easily!

Shots. Oh yeah. Expensive, but worth it if they worked. And they *did,* so long as I was taking them. "The advantage of these injections," said the teensy little nurse, "is that you lose weight while you learn a whole new set of eating habits." And you know what? Both of her predictions came true. The former—all that weight I was losing—was temporary; the latter was added to my catalogue of potential practices.

And yes. I've done Weight Watchers—successful in terms of weigh ins while I attended classes, plus exquisite recipes to add to rather than replace my repertoire. And Nutri-system. . . . Some months were required to replace the weight following that experience. Oh yes—have I introduced you to my *special* friend Jenny Craig?

Do I want to suffer? Am I playing a childish game with weight loss systems? Realize before you pick up your pen to send me a seething note that I see in retrospect what I've done. At any point, I'm only sitting down to a "good meal" or having a "quick snack." I'm not partial to sweets, and I'm no chocola-holic. I can pass up bread, and I've not eaten butter since the Twenty-first Century began. But the "meat and potatoes" of my youth, some sort of vegetable or salad, no dessert unless it's fruit—these are the standards for a meal. Not SO bad, huh? Unless we talk about "portion control."

"You have to stop going up and down like a yo-yo," my family physician told me some years ago. "Better just *be* a little heavy—women who carry a bit of weight live longer, you know. That's a scientific fact!"

I was shaking my head. If I didn't have this specter of overweight haunting me, I'd have no problems at all.

"So why not just forget it! Stop doing this to your system year after year. What's to be achieved?"

"Well . . . I was hoping that my skin will stay elastic," I told her.

She stared at me. Her spoken response was acidic. Another of my grand theories demolished.

We went to Southeast Asia to live and work. Bangkok. The odd tastes, alien aromas, drastically increased spicing—hot!—and reduced amount of meat in the diet, the mounds of vegetables and mountains of fruit . . . combined to support relaxation over diet. But in a year, almost without my realizing what was happening, I was once again chubby and well on my way toward corpulent. My appetite is nothing if not flexible.

March, April and May are sticky-rice-and-mango season in the tropics. A generous dollop of glutinous (as in *gluttony)* rice is centered on the plate, then coconut milk poured over it to soak. Petals of peeled mango (of the small, very sweet *okrang* variety) are arranged all around. The result is something that will never be listed in even the most comprehensive of calorie-counting manuals . . . a culinary calamity for fat folk. Something surpassed calorically *only* by Italy's tiramisu.

At the height of the mango season near the end of our first year, I was approaching once again the apex of my weight cycle and commiserating at work one morning with a similarly cumbrous colleague.

"You actually *want* to lose weight?" he asked.

"I'm desperate."

"I'll bet you *can't!*"

I stared at him.

"You don't like to bet?"

I was silent. I don't bet. I love to play poker, for instance, but with toothpicks or matches.

"You want to do more than *talk,* you'll bet with me!"

I have a horror of people who yak-yak-yak and don't *do.* He had my attention. "How much?"

"First, we establish the rules. Then we discuss amount."

We decided to weigh in every Tuesday morning before the work day began. If he was down a kilo (the scales at the school—as with most of the world—measured *kilos,* not the 2.2 pounds that a kilo is worth). Anyway, if he'd lost a kilo and I hadn't, I would pay him—cash in hand, not chits. Vice versa, he paid me. Neither of us down, or both down equally, no one paid anyone. And to cover all eventualities: if I (for example) held my weight while he crept up a kilo, still no one paid. Only weight *lost* a full kilo more than the other received money. And *no one* got paid for the same kilo lost again.

"All right, how *much?*" I wanted to know after we'd agreed on the guidelines.

"Well, I should tell you that I did this once before," Roger said, "and ended up subsidizing my friend's stay in Thailand at a hundred baht a kilo."

"Five dollars!" This was serious money.

Roger nodded. "Yeah, and that amount wasn't *near* enough to keep me from eating—"

"—So?"

"How about a thousand baht a kilo?"

"Fifty dollars!" I shrieked. "I don't have that kind of money!"

"That's the point," he said mildly. "Neither do I. So we both have to stop eating."

I would think about it. "Maybe after mango season . . . ?" I suggested.

He stared at me in disgust. "We record our base weight tomorrow or not at all."

Tomorrow. A thousand baht a pound. Fifty dollars! Those two ideas rattled through my head spare moments of that day and practically all of the night. Well, it's not *really* betting, I argued with myself, because weight loss is up to *me*. So we're not considering a horse at a race track or a card dealt or a number plucked from a hat. I'd have control . . . or would I? *Do I have control over what I consume?* Perhaps I should find out before I get any older.

Tuesday morning found me waiting impatiently for Roger to join me and go establish our starting weights on the scale in the nurse's office.

I'm not considered mercenary by those who know me well. But I work hard, and I like to know where my money goes. To spend it for futile purpose in penance for greed is inexcusable. There followed a year of cryptic conversations with myself when walking past a heavily-laden dessert table at a party. . . . *Have yourself a fifty-dollar brownie, Phyl! How about twenty-five bucks' worth of chocolate mousse?* Or observing a not-yet-empty serving platter on the dinner table at home: *How about a C-note's worth of satay with peanut sauce?* And for good measure I'd taunt: *Take plenty of fried rice.*

Approached that way, food was easy to pass up, and Roger's and my experiment was for me a great success. As icing on the non-existent cake, I purchased Thailand's wonderful color-stone jewelry with my "earnings." Even years later, my husband would notice a particularly beautiful opal ring on my finger and ask, "Did I get that for you, or did Roger finance it?"

One year and forty-seven fewer pounds later, my wardrobe consisted of clothing which wouldn't accommodate growth. Everything else had been cut down or donated. And the Tuesday morning weigh-in continued to provide a moment of truth that kept me gastronomically honest and physically slender for five more years in Thailand—not to mention the pleasure of continuing to spend the dollars so "earned" on my one extravagance: rings and ear rings composed of the beautifully cut color stones so very available in that country.

And when warm acquaintances and the few friends *begged* me to stop losing weight—"Phyl, you're nothing but bones anymore!"—then I knew I was getting reasonably close.

But then we left Southeast Asia and returned home to California. The first thing I noticed when I got here was the amazingly generous portions of food when eating out. Whoops! Trouble ahead. I was back in the land of prime rib and pizza, of *ice cream,* for heaven's sake. I was so astonished (and delighted) by the long-unaccustomed goodies that I forgot until too late to unpack my weight conscience. I *deserved* to taste everything, didn't I, after being deprived for all those years?

For a while, I didn't believe that overweight could happen to me again. Not after five years of habitually careful consumption and those Tuesday-morning weigh-ins. But I began playing the usual games when clothing got too tight. I'd start dieting . . . a week from next Thursday. Then I'd sigh and buy larger clothes. Once more, I reached the point of hating to look into a mirror. And oh yes, I got gooseflesh on hearing such words as *pound* and *see* and *swallow*. And once more, clothing in my closet ranged from size fourteen (all increasingly dusty) to size twenty (gradually fading from repeated laundering).

I enrolled in the various weight loss franchises one at a time, usually attained the desired goal (significantly and sufficiently less poundage) followed by the usual result afterwards (gradual weight gain).

A weight warrior along with seven of every ten adult U.S. citizens, I tried unsuccessfully for decades to win the battle permanently, "take it off and keep it off," even envisioning a minor operation or an implant (perhaps a hungry omnivore?) to increase metabolism and decrease appetite—a technological advance somewhere between cop-out and Star Trek. And it happens that remedies *are* now available . . . to those able and willing to afford the price.

I couldn't and I can't—nor am I willing to—coddle myself with such. But—gloriosa!—such remedies are no longer a factor. For about ten years, now, and for some reason that neither my long-time family doctor nor I can figure out with certainty, my appetite has diminished dramatically.

"Possibly the gall bladder removal," Dr. Archer has suggested. And yes, that's a possibility, since I no longer have the dependably automatic internal processing of fat. Nearly a decade ago, there was a spring and summer when I was not in pain—just "blah!" without energy, without appetite ("chewing" required way too much effort), without pain, and without anyone knowing what was wrong.

Finally, it was decided that the gall bladder had to go, and it went. By then, I'd lost during that period all the pounds put on since returning from Southeast Asia—and a few more besides—so that overweight became and remains since that time a painful memory, nothing more. The whole conclusion was magic!

An experienced writer, I know that "quick fixes" are no way to conclude a dilemma described in an article. But I also know that one must adhere to the truth when writing non-fiction. I'm certainly not recommending that people having a weight problem—real or imagined—should get rid of their gall bladders. But my reason for writing this, and what I remember oh so distinctly and in great detail is the experience of *being* overweight and what that perception did for too many years to my confidence and self-image.

I'm no longer a youngster, but oh the strides made in medicine during these last decades! The childhood specter of polio has virtually disappeared. Infection and disease are now assaulted successfully by remedies which are sometimes available off the shelf. Burn therapy accomplishes miracles. Certain types of cancer are no longer death decrees. Transplants are available—from hair to hearts, corneas to kidneys. Genetic engineering—if desirable—is beginning to start to commence to be possible. Stem cell potential! How about that "cloning"? Giant steps to at least *control* AIDS. Experts are working, and new thought is building on the steps climbed by past progress.

So I want to know something. Is chronic overeating such a basic character flaw that we can afford to write off more than half of the population? Drunkenness and drugs garner far more concern and sympathy. . . and medical attention! What I want to know is, *who's doing research on metabolic control* or (if that's not the basic difficulty) whatever it is that makes overweight so prevalent, regardless of who's defining the term. And this major concern is often warranted by reason of health rather than mere self-image and vanity—among females in particular. I'm not talking about "fixes"—simplistic ("Don't eat so much") or invasive ("We'll implant") this or that so that you *can't* overeat.

I'm not even going to deplore the Western male's fascination for the often unhealthy "twiggy" silhouette now becoming a "boobs and butt" approach. I merely wish that there were some way to alert the earnest and capable researchers out there who—just starting out—may be looking for a worthy arena in which they may wish to conduct their combat. Surely, a productive field to cultivate. . . . you think?

22

You Write The Music . . .

I'm slated to stay in San Diego for a month. I came down here a couple of weeks ago to first house sit and feed the cats while my son, daughter-in-law and granddaughter were in London for the opening of a stage play (that's a whole *other* story!) and then after their return I'd agreed to "stay awhile."

Define "awhile." A month is too long.

My son Shelby comes to the breakfast table on Wednesday morning. "So Mom! Can you write me some theme song lyrics for our new show?"

"Stage play for children, I presume?"

"Of course."

"You know I'd love to. What subject?

Shell clears his throat. "It's tough. You up to it?"

"Hey, c'mon! I make the words—you write the music! That's how we used to do it, no problem! Brings back 'the good old days!' Subject?"

"Pachacamac." The dancing brown eyes of my only and

185

therefore favorite son are fastened on me. Now he lowers his chin, raises his eyebrows, and peers across from below a thoughtfully furrowed fifty-year-old forehead.

"No, really, Shell! What subject?"

"Pachacamac," he repeats.

"C'mon!"

"Mom, you listening?"

Incredulous, I stare over at him. "And you want rhyme?"

He nods. "Kids love rhyme. Plus a good tight scan. We need lots of rhythm."

"Of course you do!" I study his face for a sign of jest. Nothing. "And you'll need this creation by breakfast tomorrow?"

"Three days, ok? Saturday. We pick our players that evening, hand out scripts and music."

I shake my head, pick up a pen and scrap paper. "So spell it!"

He does, then continues. "Six verses minimum——plus refrain, some kind of catchy chorus."

"LOCKIN' THE DOCK! HOCKIN' D'GLOCK!" I shake my head. And Peruvians of ancient times knew what a Glock was? And they had hock shops? "How about you create the music first—then I work from that?"

He shakes his head. "Maybe you'd like to work *with* someone?"

"No." If I'm around, I do words and Shell does music. That's how it used to be. Then he grew up—went to university. Still, summers, I did lyrics and he did notes. Then he got married, moved away, concentrated on making a living. He and his wife plus the good ol' group take off time to do a kiddy musical every spring for schools and the San Diego community.

But I still miss that old camaraderie, and there's something snugglesome about rhyming stuff—don't ask.

They're lovely and loving, Shelby and his wife Christine. (Granddaughter Louisa earns a mixed report. But what teenager's a total treasure?) However, this family has a twenty-hour daily schedule before week ends when things get *really* busy.

I tongue my dry lips. "***Pahch - uh - kah - MAHK***, right?"

Shell shrugs, nods. "Incan god, and this'll be for our Pacific Rim series."

I stare at the paper where I've written the damn syllables he gave me. No chance for misinterpretation, right? */paç -uh - kuh - MAHK /* Clear as Andes' air! "I think I remember this fellow. South American god—*pre*-Inca, wasn't he?—who created the first man and woman—but then killed the male, right?"

Shell nods. "Killed 'em both! Through oversight, that first death. Provided nothing for them to eat."

My son had been headed for his office downstairs and for his Macintosh with the scary large monitor. . . . But now he sits as I get up. He asks, "You want to discuss this?"

"No!" Clutching the paper scrap I head hurriedly for that same downstairs office. "Got me some Googling to do!"

And I do manage to get to Big Mac first.

So ***Pachacamac***——spelled several different ways in the research——was big and bold and bad and bodacious. No doubt about it. And fierce, ferocious and fatal. But I don't need alliteration for these lyrics. I need *rhyme*. For Pachacamac. All four syllables. And remember the tight scan. You betcha!

GOTCHA D'SOCK. Oh, that's useful. **COCK O' D'WALK!** Sure! Clichés are yummy.

I walk over to check the wall shelves for a rhyming dictionary. I have three such dictionaries at home. *Nada*, here, at least nothing with the regular dictionaries and thesauruses. Should that plural be "thee-sore-AYE"? My rhymers at home go up to a final three syllables, max.

But I now need *four!*

Granddaughter Louisa walks in, heads for the research section of the book wall. Ripped jeans, and her panties with a print of day-glo flowers show through a big tear around the back right pocket.

Louisa is sixteen years old, going on thirty-six, a big-city San Diego girl. An accomplished visual artist already, and a professional-for-pay island dancer—Balinese, Thai, Javanese as well as Tahitian and Hawaiian—complete with super-cascading black locks and sensational appearance. That hair inherited from her Asian mom partially covers the offending pocket.

"Honey, you want me to patch your trousers?" I can be *thinking* about Pachacamac while I do something I actually know how to do.

She turns to face me and her dark eyes bore into mine. "No-o-o!" and the drawn-out vowel ends on a rising inflection.

Danger. And oo-oo-oo, I'm so scared! Then I notice that her right fist is extending the index finger, and that finger is pointing down and bouncing. I follow the point to discover that her sneakers share the panty pattern.

"Oh, a matched set," and I nod. What a hip gramma!

She goes back to searching. "Fucking teacher wants a tri-point for display."

Ha! Language to shock Gram. I *hope* it's not typical. But I know better than to react. In fact, I *knew* better than to mention the pocket tear, but I got away with it.

"And a tri-point being . . ." My voice trails off hopefully.

She pulls a fat hard-bound from a lower shelf. *Costumes Through the Ages.* "Guess I'll Google," she mutters, "and probably end up in Wikipedia."

"So this tri-point means . . ." and I wait.

She laughs. "Taller, wider, and heavier than the artist—just kidding, ok?" She cracks up. I wonder what's funny.

"Ok, then, we're supposed to research first, right? Then we create this big visual piece of something or someone in history—oil, acrylic, mixed media, whatever—and write a report about it or him—I plan to make that a *her!* Include time and place and circumstance—then we have to list at least ten sources on the bibliography." She sighs. Life is hard.

"And oh yes, Gram! We have to display our project using some kind of technology. That's what makes it triple threat."

Sounds like a plan to me, and I am pleased that her charter high school is interdisciplinizing so creatively.

"And all this comes due . . . ?"

"—This Friday, for Open House that evening. Mom and Dad'll be there. You, too?"

I nod, then gasp. "Honey! Today's already Wednesday."

Louisa shrugs. "So long as the paint dries."

She goes, and I'm left with *Pachacamac*. **DODGIN' D'ROCK. MOCKIN' THE JOCK.** Am I on a roll, or what?

It's early Thursday morning, and I'm in the office staring at Shell's Mac and hoping for Divine Inspiration when Louisa pops in.

"Rosie the Riveter!"

I look up in wonder. It's been decades—literally!—since I've heard the term.

"She's going to be my project, Gram! I've done the research, and I took my bedroom door off the hinges this morning."

Dare I ask? "Your door's off the hinges?"

She nods. "Sure! To paint Rosie the Riveter on! I've done the sketch—you want to see?"

I nod, and she hands it over. It's Rosie all right—how does Luisa DO that!? Rosie wearing jeans, and with a smoking cigarette in her hand . . . "But—" Hoo-oo Boy, how do I say this?

"But WHAT! That's Rosie, all right! I found pictures on line."

I nod, smile, approve. . . "But she—I mean, ladies . . . uh, *women* in those days *didn't show cleavage!*" There, I've said it, and may the Good Lord have mercy on me.

"Of course they did! They were *emancipated,* Gram!"

I nod, sigh. Discretion is the better part—hell, I've never even *pretended* to be valorous. "Louisa, I was around ten years old when Rosie started 'riveting.' Second World War. Ablebodied men were in the military, and somebody had to produce the artillery and ammunition and what-all—build the tanks and planes and ships!"

"—And *women* did it! Like Rosie the Riveter."

"True. But believe me, they didn't show cleavage! They didn't even *want* to show cleavage."

"Gram, you really are so old-fashioned!"

She smiles, takes back her picture.

I smile and keep my mouth shut.

When Shell honks, Louisa leaves for her ride to school. *Rosie the Riveter with cleavage!* Lordy!

I've read that women's clothing through the ages, based on pictorial records, has always tended to cover up those portions of her body considered most sensual and arousing at that particular period. So far, and assuming that said costume theory is valid, the Twenty-first Century is pretty much *without* sensuality and arousal.

But Rosie—sure, she was temporarily out of the dishpan, away from the iron and the washing machine, even away from the stove and oven *during her workday*—but then paid dearly for that privilege during "off hours" not on the job, including the time previously utilized for sleep.

And she might smoke and wear slacks and actually draw a paycheck, but she did *not,* there in the 'Forties, expose her body. *She did not show cleavage.*

Pachacamac. **WATCHIN' D'CLOCK. MOCKIN' THE SCHLOCK.** Oh yeah, those'll fit right in!

In fact, there seems these days to be parallel terminology for heretofore secret—or at least clinical—parts of the anatomy. I laugh a little, remembering an incident which occurred while I was in charge of Student Activities and Family Information at a large international school in Thailand.

I recall that the student population that year was memorable—K-12 kids from thirty-seven different language backgrounds throughout the world! The language of instruction was English, and the classroom and administrative staff all originated in either the U.S. or England.

We were putting together a Junior-Senior High School talent show—parents participating as well as students and staff. All were encouraged to be imaginative. The only restriction was that students creating their own song lyrics must have the words first approved by me.

"What! Our sweet kids?"

But the old-timers assured me that prior approval was necessary. The school had in the past experienced problems with (shall we say) indelicate phraseology. The difficulty had resolved itself when said approval was mandated. Our school superintendent James Leland—dear, innocent old fellow that he was—agreed that such sanction might be superfluous now, "but let's stick with the plan."

So I shrugged and agreed. After all, how many kids would be making up their own lyrics?

Not many. I'd look over the printed words and indicate my consent with an initial and the date, then make a copy for the office. Eighty-five students signed for vocal-included participation, with maybe eight total presenting original songs that required vocabulary approval. . . .

No problem at all, until two days before the event when a couple of senior high boys I barely knew came through my office door and handed me a rolled sheet of vellum containing two columns of neatly typed copy.

I spread it out and got through the first verse into the chorus. Then I scanned the rest of the verses before looking up at the American kid whose name was Benjamin.

"No," I said.

"Wha-aa-at! What's wrong with it, Ms. M.?"

"You and I both know, so let's not waste each other's time, ok?"

"No, it's not ok! I always heard that you *liked* animals."

I nod. "But this isn't about an animal."

"Of course it is! What do you have against beavers?"

I shook my head slightly, then just looked at him without blinking. And believe me, I could be the poster child for "steely-eyed."

About every line in the somewhat clever wording possessed *double entendre,* and those two not only knew it but knew that I knew it. I very dispassionately read a couple of verses aloud for them:

This sweet woodland creature
Thinks maybe you'll teach her—
Show the ways of the wild
To this innocent child . . .
. . . And you DO! Oh, you DO!

To help her recover,
You tell her you love her
Don't try to deceive her—
Just ruffle her beaver. . . .
. . . And you DO! Oh, you DO!

Following a fitting pause, the other young song-writer, who now introduced himself as Lee Choi, asked a reasonable question in a reasonable voice. "Is there someone else whose approval would be acceptable in lieu of yours?"

I shrugged, nodded. "Certainly. Go talk to Superintendent Leland." Or to God.

The two nodded politely and left my office.

I tried to phone Leland, but his line was busy. We didn't have inter-office communications in the school at that time, and his secretary Sarah's line was also in service. Ok, dear innocent Dr. L., how much do you trust me?

Within ten minutes, my phone rang. Dr. Leland was whispering. "I'm in Sarah's office, and the boys are in mine. What's wrong with a beaver?"

How to explain fast. How to explain at all. I can't define the problem over the phone. And certainly not to Dr. Leland, probably not to him anywhere or ever.

After my silence, he continued, still whispering. "I take it that it has a dual meaning, and the second one is not acceptable in a public setting?"

"You take it right."

"Okay, I'll tell them 'No,' but you need to explain it to me later."

"Yes." Not in this lifetime, Sir, not to you.

I think about the incident a bit. How many of those old TV standbys might never have come about if current mentality were operant then? *Leave it to Charlie* just doesn't have the same zing.

Meanwhile: **ACH! WHATTA CROCK** and **GOTCHA M'ROCK.** Oh boy!

Open House was at the school on Friday evening—more than a dozen rooms loaded with display—all colorful and creative.

Louisa did herself proud. Standing out among other projects, her seven-foot-high bedroom door was suspended from the ceiling, dancing on the floor, bearing a gigantic Rosie the Riveter. Beautifully painted at more than life size, here was an attractive, obviously hard-working woman, sitting relaxed on a box outdoors to have a cigarette break. She wore overalls, a blue work-shirt with rolled up sleeves—and presented a most generous cleavage.

On a cup hook screwed into the unpainted left side of Louisa's illustrated bedroom door were hanging the pages of the report on Rosie atop the required Bibliography. Impressive listing—and I was quite certain that Louisa had visited no library but the book wall in her dad's office at the house. A computer is a wonderful thing!

Inserted within the hollow door somewhere was a player operable by an ivory button on the side of the door slab. You guessed it—the song emanating over and over was "Rosie the

Riveter" with a Big Band backup. And oh, I still do love the riff of an alto sax!

And speaking of music . . . It's now Saturday morning, *P-day.* Where am I with ol' Pachacamac? I gather up the accumulated envelopes and torn note paper, sort the research to put wording together, then set my fingers to the keyboard. Hmm-mm.

> Pachacamac comes out of the sea,
> The god of the fishes! How can this be?
> Here is sand, land and mountains—and sky very blue.
> He likes what he sees, and he calls it "Peru."
>
> > Pach-a-ca, Pach-a-ca, Pach-a-ca-MAC
> > Next time you come here, **we wantcha t' knock!**
> > Pach-a-ca, Pach-a-ca, Pach-a-ca-MAC!
> > You need to know that **we're watchin' d'clock!**

> He has one hundred years to stay out of the ocean.
> He'll set up his empire; at least, that's his notion.
> But *no people are here!* So then whom can he rule?
> A king with no kingdom is not very cool!
>
> > Pach-a-ca, Pach-a-ca, Pach-a-ca-MAC
> > Next time you come here, **we wantcha t' knock!**
> > Pach-a-ca, Pach-a-ca, Pach-a-ca-MAC!
> > You need to know that **we're watchin' d'clock!**

But the land is all vacant, no house and no nest—
Well, he'll take what he sees here and fill in the rest!
Time is short, but he's capable, does what he can—
He first makes a woman and then makes a man.

> Pach-a-ca, Pach-a-ca, Pach-a-ca-MAC
> Next time you come here, **we wantcha t' knock!**
> Pach-a-ca, Pach-a-ca, Pach-a-ca-MAC!
> You need to know that **we're watchin' d'clock!**

Something urgent that Pach-a does not realize—
These people need FOOD! So the man he makes dies. . . .
Now the god breaks the door down! He's strong! He can do it!
Kills their son; plants his pieces for veggies and fruit.

> Pach-a-ca, Pach-a-ca, Pach-a-ca-MAC
> Next time you come here, **we wantcha t' knock!**
> Pach-a-ca, Pach-a-ca, Pach-a-ca-MAC!
> You need to know that **we're watchin' d'clock!**

But the younger boy Wichama hides, runs away . . .
"Where?!" demands Pach-a, but Mama won't say!
So he kills her, as well, then goes out for the son.
But Wichama lives, angry, strong, on the run.

> Pach-a-ca, Pach-a-ca, Pach-a-ca-MAC
> Next time you come here, **we wantcha t' knock!**
> Pach-a-ca, Pach-a-ca, Pach-a-ca-MAC!
> You need to know that **we're watchin' d'clock!**

Pach-a still has seventy years on the land
To find that kid, kill him!—*'cause people are banned!*
But Wich's never wherever Pach-a thinks he may be—
Until Wich pushes that cruel god back into the sea!

Pach-a-ca, Pach-a-ca, Pach-a-ca-MAC
Next time you come here, **we wantcha t' knock!**
Pach-a-ca, Pach-a-ca, Pach-a-ca-MAC!
You need to know that **we're watchin' d'clock!**
Stay there in the ocean, so salty and blue—
Peru will grow strong and never need you!

(Note: diminishing volume)

Pach-a-ca,
Pach-a-ca,
Pach-a-ca,

Pach-a-ca,
Pach-a-ca
Pach-a-ca- MAC!

As it turns out, Shell finds a real Peruvian singer to play Pachacamac, a local rapper with dreadlocks that bounce off his butt. He'll put a creative spin of his own on words, thank you very much, words that he hopes come to him during each performance.

Shell asks, "D'you mind, Mom?"

"Of course not. Whatever works. I had fun with the rhymes."

"Maybe we'll use them in some other show."

"Sure. Don't worry about it. You'll do plenty more stage plays on Pachacamac."

"Right."

We both look at each other and crack up.

So now I'm packed, and I wave bye-bye to Louisa through the opening of her doorless bedroom. "Early plane, Sweetie! If I were you, I would wantcha t' knock—but you know that I gotta watchama clock! Adios!

23
·····················

The Secret is the Sorting

It was summer in 1936. I was almost five and visiting Grandma Larkin on the Kansas farm, avid to learn all mysteries linked to being grown up. There we were, washday on a Monday morning, outdoors and not far from our water source, the windmill pumping into the stock tank. A mammoth pot of water inside the house was heating on the big black range beside pans of starch and what passed for bleach on the farm in those days—bluing.

Grandma had a great drift of wavy white hair atop her head. It must have been very long, but I never did see it other than pinned. To me, always, she was an angel, and I considered that hair her halo. A born teacher, her technique was repetition. "Light delicates first, then other whites, next bright prints, darks, and finally heavy work clothes. Just remember, sorting's the secret."

Every washday, Grandma Larkin tried to impart her store of lore. I learned early on about the secrets *of* the sorting, but it took some years to learn quite independently about the secrets *in* the sorting. Grandma, who called legs "limbs" and breasts "bosoms," wasn't likely to tell me about those kinds of secrets.

I've no doubt but that she had stayed current in that way with the pocketed secrets of her offspring as she discovered them *in* the sorting. I know that—years later—I did.

I don't recall noticing until I was much older that Grandma's hands were permanently twisted and reddened. And I didn't ever consider as hardship the hours she spent on her knees bent over the wash tub scrubbing, scrubbing on that bumpy scrub board. Nor did I concern myself with the many re-washings as a consequence of bird droppings, not even the major scrubbing after a whole congress of fowl perched on the loaded lines to break their journey. To self-centered me, after all, such catastrophes meant bonus time at the tubs.

Grandma had her tools in order. A topless gallon can, containing semi-liquid lye soap she'd made last spring, was dwarfed by the three great tubs of water. The first was warm and soapy, islanded with apparel. Leaning up from inside was the wooden frame with corrugated metal, galvanized iron I sup-pose. Grandma's scrub board. Resting on the ground below the frame was a big bar of soap and a stiff-bristled brush having a water-warped handle too big for me to get my fingers around. In the second tub was what Grandma called "first rinse," some-what cloudy, a bit of soap scum bubbling around the edges but the liquid renewed often by her emptying it onto the ground and my then lugging that tub over to the pump pipe for refill and helping her drag it back to the wash area. The third tub was clear, Grandma's "last rinse."

After the final dip with possibly a short soak in bluing, perhaps a dunk in starch, I got to help wring out the garments. Then I could drag the basket load of clothes to endless wire clothesline Grandma had scrubbed earlier. What fun to hand up to her the two-pronged clothespins so that she could reach up to affix everything *just so* to dry—towels all together, table-cloths, socks, dresses, panties, blouses. And unpinning to take down? Everything smelled like sunshine and summer. Much got separated onto tidy stacks ready to sprinkle and iron, then to hang or fold and put away.

Off the farm and back home in Omaha, my parents had an electric washing machine. This noisy monster caged in the basement had an agitator to swish dirt from the fabric. An appendage *very dangerous* (they always told me) was a wringer. These two rolling bars squashed the clean clothes between them and then through first one and, following adjustment, a second tub of water before squeezing out the final rinse. Then came the bluing and/or starch, after which everything was carried outside to hang up.

I liked Grandma's arrangement better—outdoors in sparkling air, rubbing the clothes on the washboard, applying special soap and brush bristles to stains. Meantime, the windmill creaked a rhythm as it rotated in the endless Kansas wind, and one could make up laundry ditties to sing as one worked.

The wind blows squeaking blades around,
And water comes out through the pipe from the ground.

Grandma hummed along. I had a well-developed sense of rhythm and a critical ear for rhyme. The meaning of my creations wasn't all that important.

My grandmother did assure me that doing laundry in the winter was not so pleasant. "The fabric's frozen stiff by the time you get it pinned," she told me, and as I later learned first hand, at home. But I was never present in winter to help with laundry on the farm. I couldn't imagine that the whole process— concluded by *snapping* fabrics fresh off the line—could be anything other than enjoyable. Someday, I'd be grown up enough to perform this magic by myself.

Ah! . . . As the saying goes, *be careful what you wish for.*

Time passed. I grew. My Kansas grandmother left her farm and came to live with us in the "big city" in Nebraska. She took over doing laundry for my working parents. Now it was she who used the electric machine and that hazardous wringer in the basement. And she who continued educating me: the secret continued to be the sorting, and I was a willing pupil. Somehow, the appeal endured. I retained my abiding wonder at the metamorphosis of soiled clothing turning into clean apparel, pressed and hung or folded, neatly stacked in drawers. Why this great fascination? Looking back to analyze . . . here was an achievable goal, a humble matter appreciated by the family— and something that even diminutive I could accomplish.

After Grandma died when I was ten, I became the official laundress. I sorted, treated stains, blued and starched, ironed and hung or folded—and took pride in drawers neatly stacked, tidy closets with clothing ready to wear.

My father had succumbed to flu the year before. Money was tight, with the U.S. in the final throes of what would later be known as The Great Depression. My mother sold our home and bought a rooming house—seven bedrooms all upstairs with a private outside entrance separate above our five rooms of living quarters on the main floor. Seven men rented these rooms, each space with a full-sized bed, a chest of drawers, a table and chair, then a sink located under a set-in medicine cabinet. Toilets and tubs were located in two bathrooms out in the hall. Mother saw the men when they paid her the rent at the first of each month. I saw them not at all.

Because we had only fourteen sheets and fourteen pillow slips for those rooms, it was my job early on Saturday morning to collect all bedclothes, wash and dry and iron them, meantime cleaning the bathrooms and the rooms, careful to replace the linens on each bed well before dark on Saturday evening. Nebraska has a short period of daylight during winter, but the routine worked if I took stiffly frozen bed linens off the line and draped them over warm radiators indoors, then got right to the ironing. During the second winter we lived there, Mother purchased a flat-press mangle as a Christmas gift for the house, and that magical machine even finished the drying!

I was convinced (and still am) that the secret to good laundering is a matter of sorting. But it was during the five years with the rooming house that I first began to learn about the secrets *in* the sorting—well, in the *collecting* and sorting.

Tucked beneath one and another of the roomers' mattresses, falling out when I removed the bottom sheet, would be a magazine or even a whole book with pictures such as I had never seen or imagined. Girls. Women. Dressed. Undressed. The pictures were of no great interest beyond my surprise that they *existed*. But the bit of text provided considerable education for a ten-year-old. Intense interest for a twelve-year-old. And fascination for a fourteen-year-old. I smuggled the publications down to the basement washing machine, read fast, read everything—and returned all to the spots that had spawned them, good as new. The supply was replenished frequently, and the variety seemed to be unlimited.

Also, rooms One and Five, upstairs, usually had a cache of brightly designed little packages falling out from under the mattress when I collected sheets. They all had the word "prophylactic" somewhere in the labeling. This word was unfamiliar to me, but I had the strong feeling that I shouldn't ask. Brought up in the Baptist church, I had a well developed instinct about what was and what was not appropriate to inquire about. I knew very well, for example, that the reading material found under the mattress was to be enjoyed but never mentioned. I now consulted the household dictionary only to learn that *prophylactic* meant "preventative" and had to do with protecting from disease. But why would someone keep medicine under his mattress and not in the medicine cabinet?

I didn't dare to open a sealed package for inspection, and I didn't know whom to ask about them. Certainly not my mother, and absolutely not the owners of these enticing packages. Nor did my friends, as it turned out, know any more about them than I—so *who?*

No one. My imagination bubbled. Inside each packet was a delicious chocolate bon-bon? But regrettably squishy, melted, as the content always seemed soft. No, wait. How about a tiny yo-yo, for I could feel the wound string circled inside. What*ever* might be contained in these mysterious and oh-so-tightly-sealed packages?

In all, I found the task of changing sheets for our roomers far more exciting than the weekly linen exchange downstairs. When I went away to college, Mother sold the rooming house. But one year in an all-girls' school let me learn about prophylactics and a great number of other matters which I had and even had *not* wondered about before.

Grown now, married with two children, laundering turned out to be the one thing about managing a household that came naturally. And more secrets *in* the sorting were discovered as my youngsters became more independent.

Wherever did you get this pocket stuffed full of Walnettos? Next came my surreptitious phone call to the manager of the local grocery followed by a carefully-counted-out removal from the piggy bank, then a sober trudge to that store, a tearful confession by my four-year-old followed by the agreed-on lecture by a Big Man. Payment for the pilfered goodies accompanied their return. A lesson learned. My son at age fifty says he still remembers his one excursion into thievery. And: *This note about your classmate that I found in your pocket? It's unkind and inappropriate.* My third-grade daughter discussed with her mother some ways to make amends. Even more discoveries among stains and pocket contents for my teenagers. Secrets *in* the sorting!

"Do women go to some kind of a laundering school?" That was my late husband Ivan questioning Jenny, a long-time friend from Thailand, now returning to the States and staying with us in northern California before she purchased property of her own. I was temporarily out of town, and Jenny had stepped up to get the wash taken care of in my absence.

Stunned by the question, Jenny just stared at the man, then shook her head. "Of course not."

"But—" he was mystified. "You fold exactly the same as Phyl—you two even *sort* alike!"

Jenny's a joker, straight-faced, outrageous. "Women's intuition—you've heard of that?"

An educated man, Ivan placed "women's intuition" in a category with werewolves and vampires, so he abandoned the subject.

Jenny told me about the exchange weeks later. "You'll remember," she concluded, "I worked in Southeast Asia for seventeen years. Like you when you lived there, I had a housekeeper who did it all. Coming back, I knew I was on my own for everything domestic. So I watched —*very* closely—how you laundered and folded, how you loaded the dishwasher, used the vacuum sweeper, dusted—everything!"

We both got a good laugh and were prepared to confess all to Ivan, but he never brought up the subject again to either of us. I presume that he was still bewildered when he went to his grave.

More than seven decades from those days with Grandma on the Kansas farm, I am in my household the undisputed Queen of Laundry. Nor is anyone apprenticing, so far, despite my frequent hints. As a parent and now a grandparent in our extended family, and unlike Grandma Larkin, I am a failure in the arena of imparting my expertise.

But as queen, I have issued a few commands. First, *zip up.* Half in the family do; half don't. So I go through the sort zipping up jeans rather than needing to mend the fabric bites from ravenous metal teeth. The second dictate: *empty the pockets.* How is it that one little tissue left in clothing can create a thousand bits of white fluff on every article sharing the dryer? So yes, I go through every pocket of every garment. The advantage to this procedure—and all have fair warning of my practice—is that I keep for myself all monies discovered in these recesses. I drop the change and even cash into a jar sequestered in the laundry room. Well, I do have a self-imposed limitation. . . . If a pocket produces more than twenty-five dollars, I return the cash to its owner. That's happened twice. Usually, we're talking about a dime or a few pennies.

Three years ago, I was preparing to take a trip to Africa. The round trip airfare (coach, yet!) was half the cost of everything needed for a whole month in Zimbabwe. So I searched all hidey-holes where I squirrel away change and currency "just in case." (Remember, I'm a "Depression" kid.) The laundry jar yielded $104.37—not bad for eleven years of collecting from pockets.

Granddaughter Sultana, who is the teenage queen of *creating* laundry at our house, is presently away at college and insists that I "teach her" to launder. Sure, you bet! But whenever three minutes pass without producing total enlightenment, she has disappeared.

I recently spent thirty-four days visiting my son and his family at the other end of the state. When I got home, I had awaiting my return at least half as many loads of laundry as I'd spent days away. It's nice to be needed. When I am gone and laundry has reached the *truly* critical stage at home, my daughter will grudgingly step up. But then she puts her husband's work jeans in with Sultana's sequined camisoles. I noted this morning three bleach spots on my daughter's blue blouse, doubtless a result of her own laundering effort. I attempted to explain the simple trick of bleaching with a single rinse the few sturdy (and only the *white)* fabrics needing such a remedy. "Then you drain and rinse, leave them in the washer, and put in the rest of the non-delicate lights and do the whole double-rinse cycle without Clorox."

"Oh, Mom! Write about it in your will!"

The thing is, I have a busy life apart from laundry. But although *I* know that the secret of laundry is the sorting, others in my household consider that truism an old wives' tale. My laundering skills are taken for granted. Actually, what I'm best *known* for is an ability to remove stains. And the word gets around. Friends and the occasional neighbor bring in from time to time some prized article of clothing flawed by a stubborn blot. A long-time friend once mailed me a spotted piece of batik from Thailand. And a few months back, I got in the post from an acquaintance in Manila an embroidered shirt of coconut fiber, his treasured *barong tagalog,* marked "indelibly" by ballpoint pen. Doesn't everyone know by now that a cheap, high-lacquer hairspray takes care of ballpoint ink?

But never mind. Grandma Larkin would approve, for I still do get that old thrill from sorting out and doing laundry and especially, over the years, from removing a stain without hurting the fabric. Go figure!

24

While I was Dead

On Friday in mid-April, my husband died with little pain and great dignity. The charge nurse at the hospital told me, "You need to call Social Security."

I nodded.

Then our long-time doctor hugged me. "You ok?"

Not really trusting my voice, I murmured, "This was . . . no surprise."

"But we're never really ready."

I nodded again.

She squeezed my hand with both of hers. "Soon as possible—early next week will do—phone Social Security."

"Social Security," I repeated as she disappeared down the hallway.

Then the funeral home counselor gave me a "To Do" list containing a bolded toll-free number with "SOCIAL SECURITY" in all caps.

I dialed the 800 number on Tuesday and went through a series of automated voices until a human tone reached my ear. "How may I help you?"

Identifying myself, I told her the situation.

"No notification yet," she said. "You need to mail in a death certificate immediately."

"The funeral home promised a death certificate within ten working days."

"But you called here anyway?" An edge in her voice.

"I was told—by everyone—to call you as soon as possible."

"You say your husband died last Friday. This is Tuesday. That's 'as soon as possible'?"

I let my breath out slowly. "Yes."

She asked several routine questions about address and phone. Then: "Was this a first marriage?"

"Second, for both of us."

Silence.

"But long-standing. Thirty-two years."

More silence. Then, "Two prior divorces?" Disapproving. She asked for and I supplied the date of my divorce and the date of our subsequent marriage. Then, "And the date of your recently deceased husband's divorce?"

"I don't know."

"You don't *know* the date of your husband's divorce? Yet you married him?"

More deep breaths by me. "Yes. More than thirty years ago. I may have known once, but not now. Is—is it important?"

"Madam, I do not ask *un*important questions! Now, the date of his divorce . . . ?"

"—Would have been well before we met. He and his former wife lived a thousand miles apart—and had for years."

"I cannot believe that you don't know the date of your husband's divorce."

My face heated. I felt embarrassed, guilty, stupid. But then I thought, *How many second wives remember many years later a date unimportant to them in the first place?* Tears were dropping onto my stack of papers, but I resented the tone of this disembodied voice coming across the line. I decided to speak up.

"You know, ma'am, people who make this kind of call aren't in the best spirits, anyway. And when you scold and find fault—well—it's unpleasant."

Dripping sarcasm, "I am *so* sorry to wound your delicate sensibilities—"

My jaw clenched. "What is your name, please?"

Pause. "Carolyn."

"Well, Carolyn, I think I'll hang up now and call later to talk to someone else."

"But we're practically finished."

"We *are* finished, Carolyn."

"This is dumb, lady. Only about ten more questions—*why?*"

"Because I prefer a civil—uh—thank you." My shaking hand put down the receiver. Two hours later, I phoned again and started over. This time, my courteous agent was not unduly disturbed when I confessed to not knowing, more than three decades after the fact, the date of my husband's divorce. She tried to find, but located nothing on line about the earlier Social Security phone conference.

My first clue that something was amiss came when I went for a scheduled doctor's appointment a few weeks later. "You're not listed on Medicare anymore," the secretary told me. She double-checked, then contacted my HMO.

"That person is deceased." I heard the words clearly across the line.

"But she's here, talking to me right now," the secretary protested.

Secure Horizons, however, was adamant.

Confused, I canceled my appointment "until we get things straightened out."

At home, I tried to inform Medicare but could get no human voice, and the nature of my query fitted none of their automated categories. When I myself phoned the HMO, the agent was confident that I had died in April.

"My husband did, but not me. I'm talking to you right now."

"We have no way of knowing who's talking to us. Medicare has the woman as deceased."

"Look, I'll come to your office and prove who I am, and you can make a copy of my husband's death certificate and get the record right."

"Not here. It's Medicare you have to convince."

"So where's Medicare actually located?"

"I have no idea."

A few days later arrived a letter from Social Security addressed "To the Survivors of . . ." me.

Since I could find in the phone book no local phone number, I had that mailing in hand when the Social Security office opened the next morning.

"Let me check." The pleasant worker punched some keys, frowned, punched some more, then swiveled to face me.

"You are recently deceased."

I nodded. "And yet, here I am—talking to you."

She grinned. "Can you prove it's you?"

Deliberately loaded with identification, I could and did. "And your husband?"

I gave the name and presented the death certificate.

"A mix-up. According to the record, he's alive."

"Can you correct the record?"

"I can try." She didn't sound as hopeful as I might have wished.

There followed weeks of mail addressed to my "survivors"—and of my going daily to the Social Security Office. It opens at nine, weekdays only. I was first to snap a number off the machine by the door.

"Yesterday," I told the attendant, "my family got papers to sign so they get the close-out on my life insurance. And you know that I presently have no health insurance, no Social Security check, no teaching pension."

"We've corrected the record at this office," the sympathetic woman told me, "but Medicare doesn't want to change—and it's that record people check."

Days passed. I watched Social Security employees open their service window, see omnipresent me waiting there, and walk away to be replaced by some agent who, presumably, had less tenure. I was pleasant. Patient. But also persistent—especially for a cadaver—and I was a perpetual reminder that all was not well with The System.

I heard one agent talk to State Teacher Retirement in Sacramento. "This office certifies absolutely that she is alive, apparently well, is in fact standing before me."

She hung up. "I think it worked, for now. Nothing's going to help if we can't get Medicare to respond."

"You're good," I told her. "You think you could convince my HMO?"

She just looked at me.

213

I thanked her and left, the morning routine complete. No money had come into my bank account for more than three months.

My doctor's office was calling several times a week. "Phyl, we need to know you're okay. Just come in."

"Not until I have insurance. I'm fine physically, not depressed, just baffled. And I'm staying busy, believe me. Don't worry."

The physician herself called. "Come for a chat—old friends, no charge."

My pride is almost tangible. I don't rack up bills I may not be able to pay, and I don't take charity. Besides, what if something *were* wrong physically? "I'll call when I have insurance."

One thing was certain: I had to get some kind of job. Substitute teaching was the most logical and immediate possibility. That had been my profession for forty-five years before retiring. So I called, took in papers and TB clearance to several districts, and was informed that because of recent national events (this was 2001), I now needed my fingerprints in the federal file.

No problem. I made an appointment at the county sheriff's office. Gone are the days when officers ink up your fingers and roll them across white paper. Now it's high tech—and the deputy charged with the task couldn't get prints from my fingers clear enough that the computer would accept them. She passed the task to others, who oiled and talcumed and soaped variously but to no avail.

One held my fingers up to the light and examined them one by one. "They're kind of smooth," she told me, "and a lot of the whorls are broken." She tried again. Nothing. "Look, the regular technician is off today. She can get prints off a billiard ball. Could you come back first thing tomorrow morning?"

I could and did, despite the eighty-mile round trip. A confident deputy laughed about the inexpert efforts of her predecessors. *"Every*one has fingerprints," she assured me. But after eight or ten tries, she too was mystified. "Did you ever sand off your prints for some reason?" she asked.

I laughed. "My fingers have been very busy for a long time," I told her. "Oh, and I also did stained glass for years. Lots of cuts, I suppose."

"You have no prints left."

"But I *have* to have something on file!"

She shook her head, shrugged.

I drove home close to despair. *I* thought I was still alive, even though the system didn't. But now—without fingerprints—should I just close my eyes and stop breathing and make all cyberspace giddy with joy? On impulse, I stopped in at the local school district office in Chico and explained my dilemma.

"Ridiculous!" the clerk told me. "Here, I'll phone the university." And she did. I was not hopeful three days later when I walked in for my appointment and saw the very same type of ornery machine which had eschewed my fingers in the adjacent county. Especially when a snip of a student who looked twelve years old announced that she was the technician. Should I warn her that I'd had previous problems with this big black creature? That I was officially *dead?*

But I simply smiled and murmured, "Good luck."

She got acceptable prints on her first try. My fervent "Thank You!" made her raise her eyebrows. Now I could earn enough to tide me over until Medicare and the pension and health insurance got sorted out. Ok, Federal System—you're going to owe me *so much money* and maybe even an apology.

Soon, I had insurance through Blue Shield, a company which took its agent's word—as he stood facing me in our living room—that I did indeed exist. That important fact apparently seeped into Medicare records, as well. Within a few weeks, my pension arrived at the bank—in fact several months' worth—along with Social Security.

The phone call from Secure Horizons came late one afternoon. "Mrs. Phyllis J. Manning?" A bouncing voice filled with enthusiasm.

"Yes."

"Mrs. Manning, I have terrific news for you."

"Oh?"

"Your health insurance is reinstated—retroactively!"

"Retroactively," I echoed.

"Isn't that wonderful?" All resonant with good cheer. "Your insurance is back, and it's *retroactive!*"

"But—why would I want it retroactive? I already canceled doctor appointments."

"But Ma'am! Reinstated retroactively. *As if it were never gone!*"

I thought of the dozen or so hours I'd spent on the HMO line waiting, waiting, waiting for a human voice—only to be told that there was nothing to be done or—twice—that the workday was now concluded, and would I like to try again tomorrow? And this woman had simply touch-toned my number and here we were talking.

"Can you give me one single advantage *to me* in what you're offering? I now have insurance with another company."

Silence.

Then it struck me: what a scam! "You've been taking automatic deductions from my checking account? Even though I had no insurance—no need for it since you insisted that I was dead—you took the money, anyway?"

"An error. Two separate parts of our company. But now that you're reinstated *retroactively*—"

"—*No* reinstatement! Retroactively or otherwise! And please refund every penny you took from my account after mid-April."

"But our insurance—"

"—Was getting more expensive every quarter. May I expect a refund check within this next week?"

"That's too soon—"

"—All right, I'll wait *two* weeks before I contact my attorney."

As if I had an attorney. . . . But the woman agreed and the refund actually did arrive in a mere twelve days.

That was it, then. I was officially back among the living with Medicare and Social Security and all of the agencies that follow their lead. I had health insurance, now, and pension money coming in—and daily jobs substitute teaching besides, as many as I wanted.

I had learned a valuable lesson, too: *don't ruffle the feathers of a federal bird with pecking capability.*

All through this ordeal, I believed that the matter would be funny in retrospect—sure, *black*ly humorous, but amusing nevertheless. Medicare never did apologize. Still, after that final phone call from the HMO, I felt Alive at Last. Still, it's taken some time for the laughter to come, and I'll always believe that the mix-up was caused deliberately by that coot who called herself "Carolyn."

25

(New Hebrides: Malekula)

And here, a true tale of my (only?) Notable Antecedents:

A Pistol In Her Pocket

Osa and Martin Johnson believed in hunting animals with film rather than bullets. In venturing to obscure places, they document-ed locations which in the early Twentieth Century most travelers would never see. They pioneered photography of indigenous people and of wildlife in natural settings. They worked while radio was in its infancy, movies were without sound—and TV was a wild sci-fi dream. This daring pair did then-popular lecture circuits to finance their travels but were frequently on the edge of bankruptcy. Touring the States and Europe, they used still photos certainly, but especially amazing cinematic footage exposed and developed by Martin in the field.[11]

Although much of their later work occurred in remote parts of Africa, here is an account of their first adventure together: "on location" in the South Seas.

---

[1] See (VHS) *Simba* and also the contemporary sound films (DVD) *Across the World, Baboon, Borneo, I Married Adventure,* and *African Paradise.*

Osa Johnson clung to the gunwales of the eighteen-foot whaleboat. The trades were brisk this morning, the bay water rough. This was it, finally, she and Martin far from Kansas. . . . Far in time, following six years of dreaming and planning and scrimping. They had been focused from the start. Not many months after she had come out as a debutante, and to the consternation of her family, Osa Leighty of Chanute, Kansas, married when she was sixteen. Parental concern had to do not with her age but with the man selected. The groom was only son to a very solid family—his father being a well-established jeweler in Independence, Kansas. But Martin himself was not all that stable, as they viewed him, traipsing off on adventures all over the world and then trying to make a living as a lecturer on the subject of these travels. . . . He'd even spent months with those wandering Londons aboard the *Snark.* What sort of life could their well-bred and gentle daughter look forward to?

Certainly the young couple had traveled far geographically, to be here in this boat at this place on this day. They were in the New Hebrides, due east of Cairns in Australia's tropical Queensland, well north of New Zealand. They were traveling among bits of land in the Southwest Pacific, one of the many remote places Martin had selected as little known and therefore ripe for exploration. A "fur piece," as farmers back home in Kansas termed this place.

The young woman twisted her head back to see the receding little isle of Vao. This had been their brief stopover while in the care of long-time missionary resident Father Prin. On that tiny piece of land were five hundred "tame" natives, as the population was described in Cairn. Best to headquarter there, the young couple was advised. No one in Australia offered or was asked to define *tame*. . . . An oversight born of ignorance,

Osa knew now. Even during their brief five days on Vao of set-tling in and getting organized, she and Martin both had seen the eerie knobs carried so proudly by handles of swinging hair. These *tame* Vaotians at some time recently—if not actually now in modern 1917—had truly loved their enemies. Preferably me-dium well done.

Martin leaned back. "You have your pistol, Ohsie?"

She nodded, smiled, patted her pocket. Much good it would do her. Martin was oh so proud to give it to her as a gift when they left Jack London and Charmian in Hawaii to start west on this first filming trip together. Oh, he had shown her how to insert the .41 caliber shells and how to cock the hammer of the two-shot derringer weighing less than a pound.

"But why will I *need* it?" she asked her husband. "We're shooting film, not guns—and this wouldn't stop an elephant."

"It wouldn't even stop a monitor lizard," Martin had laughed. "But a monitor isn't going to attack. Neither is an el-ephant, if we keep our distance. This is self-defense only, my dear. Anything dangerous that gets too close."

How will I know what's "dangerous"? And how close is too close? She had tucked the weapon into her pocket and prayed si-lently that she would never need it. Well, a snake. Any snake she could see would be *too close.* But she'd have to overcome that ter-ror before Martin ever discovered it. And she simply could not confess that she didn't know how to shoot—had never wanted to learn. Certainly she could not have admitted such a thing in front of Charmian London, who could do *all* things well. Then in the time aboard ship coming out, Osa had procrastinated. It would never occur to Martin that a Midwestern woman would know nothing of a gun. Osa was the daughter of gentle folk. Well, yes. But Osa was a tomboy and a rebel.

"I'll learn to shoot," she whispered to herself for the thou-sandth time in the last three months.

But what if her life on this very day depended on that pistol? What if everyone's did? Was Martin carrying a firearm? She knew that their six bearers did not. Father Prin had advised her husband against putting any kind of weapon in the hands of helpers until they proved themselves. The missionary priest considered himself a *realist*, for he had made only seventeen converts during his thirty years here on tiny Vao.

Osa noticed that they were sailing parallel to the west coast of big Malekula—the land of forty thousand **un**tamed people. Prin had tried to talk them out of coming here.

"Their big Chief Nagapate is a terror," the priest warned. "Intelligent—shrewd, fiendish, with a predilection for long pig."

"Long pig?" Osa looked to Martin, who returned her glance with raised eyebrows and a nod. Oh yes, she remembered the South Sea Island pidgin-speak for human flesh.

The priest was unable to discourage Martin, whose integrity required him to photograph the real thing. His protest: "Taking pictures of Vaotians instead of Malekulans would be like substituting zoo animals for those in natural habitat." Nor was the worried little priest able to prevent Osa's accompanying her husband. On that matter she was adamant—and Martin had promised before their journey began that she could go where he went. He already regretted making the commitment, she knew; but he would keep his word and she would fiercely hold him to it.

Despairing at last, Father Prin gave them one piece of advice for their work in a south sea wilderness: "Smile at people, no matter what—and *never* smile at wildlife." Osa presumed that Martin grasped the meaning, for her husband nodded and chuckled. She did not, and to ask would expose her ignorance. She felt as if she teetered on a quivering rail, trusting luck and pluck—and of course Martin—to see her through until she gained the balance she was determined to acquire.

They beached their borrowed boat at Tanamarou Bay, said by the priest to have the overgrown but only trail up into country containing Nagapate's fierce tribes called "Big Numbers," Martin's avowed objective. The deserted and trackless sand above a small bay was walled on three sides by trees so high and heavy as to appear more black than green—and so moist that humidity steamed. Bearers set the crate of gifts above the high water line, and the party of ten clustered by it to look around and swat insects. Buzzing mosquitoes circled Osa's head, and she tasted the salt of perspiration when she nervously licked her lips. She had not known what to expect when they arrived, but it wasn't this . . . not this false isolation. She could *sense* concealed strangers beyond their small group . . . *No,* she told herself. *Only your fancy!* The forest pressed too close. She shivered, in spite of the heat.

"Find a trail," Martin told the men. "We leave the crate here until we move inland."

"But shouldn't we hide the box?" Osa asked. And when Martin did not respond, "So we can use it when we find people?"

"It's as safe here as anywhere, sweetheart."

"No one . . . ?" The contents represented quite a lot of their scarce money. "I mean, someone could—"

"—C'mon, Ohsie, remember?" He laughed. "These people are not civilized. They don't steal."

Ah yes, the legendary honesty. They bury their old grandparents alive. They kill and eat people taken in battle, shrink their heads and carry them about as trophies or store them in head houses used to make magic. Yet are too honorable to take something which is not theirs. . . . Perhaps Osa would believe this honesty when she saw it for herself.

"Why, remember in Bora Bora when Jack London and I—"

"—We should probably find a trail soon, don't you think?" Osa asked brightly. She didn't want to hear about Martin's high adventures with the Londons because she'd already heard everything dozens of times in her husband's lectures. . . . True, but not the whole truth. She tried to be honest with herself. With Martin as well, in most situations, but not this one. She was frankly jealous—of his time spent with the Londons before she became part of his life, yes, but she was *especially* jealous of Charmian. The woman was a thorough delight, possibly Osa's favorite woman in the world, and certainly Osa did not consider herself a jealous sort—but Charmian London could handle any weapon and withstand any hardship, could navigate by the stars . . . could cook up a five-course meal from a few fish and some sargasso weed, so Martin assured her. Osa knew first hand that Charmian said exactly the right thing in any situation, had a wonderful sense of the ridiculous, was knowledgeable about everything—yet an attentive listener . . . and she kept a tight rein on her temper. In these last, Osa considered herself lacking, a fact that made someone like Charmian hard to accept. Yet, Osa loved and admired the older woman—who could resist Charmian London?

Never mind, Osa told herself as the bearers searched the tree line for a path. I'm surely prettier, at least younger, exceptionally smart and ready to—no, *determined* to learn. Even to shoot a gun—*especially* to shoot a gun! Martin chose *me*, not someone else. She observed with pride her tall, handsome husband as he stood clutching their only movie camera. That strong cleft chin! He's powerful enough for both of us at the moment, she mused. And within a few months, he will depend on me and trust me fully in any situation. Oh, he *will!*

The men returned without locating a trail. Everyone gathered by the crate, tiny Osa able to crouch in its shade. Martin busied himself with sorting and selecting camera equipment. "It is likely," he said, "that a Big Numbers tribesman is watching us at this moment."

Probably several, Osa thought but did not say. *And all licking their chops.* Like the bearers, though, she peered along the jungle wall with apprehension. What they all spied at last was a hideous little man trotting toward them across the sand. He was naked and filthy, wizened as a prune. His face was distorted, and both hands with fingers splayed clutched his stomach as he came forward.

"My word!" he said as he stopped in front of Osa. "Belly belong me walk about too much!"

My stomach is distressed. Osa glanced over at Martin, and both bit back laughter. So many warnings to stay clear of this wild Malekula Island with its forty thousand *un*tamed natives, each capable of dealing death to an intruder—only to be met by one grimy goblin speaking the very South Sea *patois* that she with Martin had been learning aboard ship coming out. Before them stood a gnome with a bellyache!

Osa dug into her ready kit and removed a dozen cascara tablets, indicated through jerky pidgin and mime that he should take half the pills before he slept, the other half in the morning. She was proud of her message, pleased with the man's patience as she fumbled for words. Finished at last, she handed him the pills. He promptly devoured them all.

"Can they hurt him?" Martin asked.

"Doubt it." She tried to keep her voice calm like his, not shaking with mirth.

"Good thing you explained the dosage," he said.

Still holding his middle with one hand, the man smiled, swept his arm to indicate that all of them should follow him.

Martin was grinning as the eight entered deep shade to follow their leader up a steep trail previously invisible and now treacherous with slimed leaves. Osa was apprehensive. Here was the grand unknown she had dreamed of and struggled so hard to experience. She had not included in her reveries the anxiety which now threatened to overtake her. . . . *Martin must not sense her trepidation.*

"Could have waited *weeks* to get an invitation like this," he murmured with satisfaction as he carried the big movie camera in its canvas hood. A bearer held the open tripod at the ready, as Martin requested, so that no good shot would be missed. Other men carried still cameras and lighting equipment. Puffing pairs took turns in hefting the loaded crate up the perilous path.

Up, up the winding trail they all went. No air stirred beneath the canopy far overhead, and the exertion of the climb left everyone wet, perspiration darkening even the top layers of Osa's long skirts.

At last, they reached a clearing. Treetops still shaded them, and giant split-leaf philodendrons soared up along trunks and tendrils to right and left. But knee-high grass replaced knotted underbrush here, and the trail seemed to disappear. For several moments, nothing and no one but themselves seemed to occupy the area. Here was a time to catch much-needed breath.

Then people emerged, mostly men much larger than their guide, all silent, wearing broad-strip pandanus-leaf skirts, for the most part, but some wearing nothing, a semi-circle of humanity at the edges of the clearing.

And suddenly, there *he* was, without doubt: Chief Nagapate—every bit the mammoth and forbidding reality which launched legends and spun rumors. The human bone inserted through the cartilage of his nose seemed larger than those worn by his tribesmen. And the great bush of hair and beard seemed somehow wilder, adding to his magnitude and menace. Unmistakably the leader, this one—even a casual observer would spot him. Osa's smile turned brittle but stayed frozen on her face. *Smile at the people but not at the predators.* How does one define *predator*?

Nagapate came toward them slowly and with great dignity and assurance. Osa could not read his deeply etched features. She realized gradually that the *whir-rr-rr* of Martin's camera beside her had been going for some time. Even while fiery brands rained on his head, her husband would film Armageddon!

Martin kept his right arm steadily grinding while the great chief stopped before the camera and put his index finger on it lightly, then drew back scowling at the vibration. He tried touching it once more, pulled away. Osa stepped forward. No women were here—did that mean they were being protected or that they counted for too little? Well, Martin was busy. She lifted her chin to eye Nagapate fully. Like it or not, female or no, the chief would have to deal with her.

Watching her narrowly, head cocked, the big man approached, then stuck out his greasy paw to grasp her forearm. Osa kept smiling, tried not to tense at his touch.

"Too close there for a good shot, Sweetheart," came Martin's soft, calm voice. "Try to work him to your left as I change the camera angle."

Oh yes, my dear husband, Osa thought. *You want profile first, then full face? A little mouth movement for you to fill in speech for your lectures?* She moved slowly as he bade, the chief following, his hand still on her arm. Osa stifled a shudder.

The big man continued to clutch her arm too firmly for her to ease away but not so tightly as to cause pain. Now he handed his club to a man nearby and proceeded with the fingers of his freed right hand to rub at the skin of her forearm. The motion was gentle only at first. At last he spat on the reddening skin and rubbed vigorously, watching her pale arm turn bright pink.

He finally stopped, looked down into her face, tossed his head and released his grip. "Skin belong Mary like fish." But then his hand immediately went to her dark brown hair, rubbing at it with thumb and index finger as he held a swatch on the top of her scalp. *Think of something else, Osa. He's not hurting you.* Hair! She had far too much of the stuff, she knew, cascading in waves to her waist. She'd wanted to cut it, make it easier to wash and care for, but Martin liked it long.

Well, this settles it. Here is good reason to clip it. She was no longer the silly, vain society miss of Chanute, Kansas. Nor not ever again! She was Mrs. Martin Johnson: proud. Growing stronger with each moment. True, she had further still to go than she'd already come. She was cataloguing silently the improvements she must make in herself when suddenly she gave an involuntary yelp as Nagapate yanked on the tress he held.

Osa swallowed, put the smile back on her features. "It's all mine," she told him brightly, "and it's attached."

"Good girl!" Martin said with satisfaction. *Whirr-rr-rr,* went the camera. "Relax, dear. No one here takes scalps."

Right. Heads, yes, but not scalps. And no one steals. "May I show anger?" she gritted to Martin through the side of her still-smiling mouth.

"If he becomes obnoxious, yes—in fact, do! He may interpret anything less as weakness."

The chief had both hands at her hair now, one to hold the tresses aside, the other to poke at her scalp.

"Is this sufficiently obnoxious?" she asked her husband.

He laughed. "The man is merely curious, my dear. You're doing well."

"Big bush belong Mary," Nagapate said finally, as he dropped her hair and stepped away.

Osa felt a shiver of relief go through her. His second utterance. Pidgin—yes! Any female in these islands was called "Mary," just as "Sheila" was the term for females in Australia. Perhaps Martin and she could someday truly communicate with these people. . . . Perhaps they would live to do so. She looked Nagapate in the eye, returned his vast grin.

"Try the gifts." Martin's voice came evenly, blending with the grind of his camera.

Does nothing bother him? She nodded, walked to the unopened box, motioned a bearer to use the dull side of his bush knife and pry up the boards.

She lifted out lengths of brightly printed cotton, looked at the silent Nagapate, held out several folded packets to him. The man's face sobered as he touched and inspected the material, then frowned over at her without comprehension. She patted the fabric of her own skirt. His eyes widened, and he dropped the cloth in disgust. *Worthless?* She picked it up carefully to show that although useless to him it did indeed have value. The smile stayed on her face as she replaced the material in the crate and drew out strings of beads. She had seen no women, yet, nor any children either. She would be more comfortable offering jewelry to them.

She placed one strand on her own neck, held out the remaining strands to Nagapate.

He laughed, and his men joined in. His other hand came up to fling the necklaces away. *Again without importance.*

"You're extremely rude," she told him softly, still smiling, holding back outrage and knowing he could not understand her rebuke. For once, she told herself as she bent to retrieve the beads, be a little patient. My goodness, these people probably haven't ever owned anything more than coconut shells, maybe a clay pot or two, some cowries? How could they understand intrinsic value?

"Try tobacco." His camera still churning, Martin's suggestion came in a subdued voice.

She turned back to the box, but hesitated. "He'll only throw it down, get it dirty."

Martin snorted. "You underestimate the influence of whalers and sailors, my love. . . . Go on, he'll know what it is."

"Mm-mm." But what if he didn't? How would he respond to three unacceptable offerings? Her hands shook as she dug deeply into the sides of the crate and pulled up tobacco in various forms. *Now, husband, shall I demonstrate its use? Perhaps a good chaw tucked up in my cheek?*

But *Ah*'s of recognition echoed among the tribesmen. With an eager smile, the chief held out both hands to collect the packets as quickly as she retrieved them.

"And you are so very welcome!" she told him cordially as he stuffed into the waistband of his pandanus skirt everything she could find to give. *Why does it not simply fall through to the ground?*

With great shuffle and show, Nagapate stomped over among the men to distribute what Osa could see was but a small portion of his booty. Martin kept grinding as a murmur began to rise from the natives. Were they dissatisfied with their leader's disbursement? Well, that was between them and Nagapate, not her affair nor Martin's. She motioned the bearers to replace the lid on the trade box. She would hope to find a village and distribute what remained.

A drum *boomed* not far from their clearing. Osa fought the shudder which native percussion gave her at various ports en route to this place and especially over on Vao. This hesitating, inconsistent beat, this *non*-rhythm, was used, Father Prin had told them, to communicate over miles. The regular cadence, he had said, was practiced close up for dance and entertainment. But these drums included beats at a distance, patchy, talking privately. *Dangerous?* The men assembled at the edges were looking at each other, then at their leader, restless. Osa felt increasingly wary, alert.

She realized suddenly that Martin too sensed danger in the drumming. He would know far better than she. He had ceased to photograph, smoothly folded up the tripod, handed it to one of his men. Now he directed with motions above the growing din for the bearers to pick up the trade crate. He would entrust the precious camera to no one but himself. Without seeming to hurry, he wrestled the canvas cover on rapidly. Osa sensed his urgency, though, and she prickled to the changing mood around them. Nagapate had satisfied his curiosity, had received the gifts he valued. *But now what?*

*Boom . . . boom-**boom**-boom.* The number of natives had increased threefold at least. More men slipped out from between the trees with each passing moment, all eyeing their visitors.

"Go first down the trail," Martin said, iron in his tone.

Why? But she turned to do his bidding.

*Boom-**boom**!*

"Step lively!" he urged.

She trotted down the path, slid on rotting vegetation.

*Boom-**boom** . . .boom!*

"You still have your pistol?" Martin asked.

She nodded as she increased her pace. Now loping down the incline, she pulled the pistol from her skirt pocket. Offered it back behind her without slowing. He took it.

Next came a deep roar from many voices above. Perhaps by now a hundred. Then a thundering vibration. Nagapate and his men were coming!

*Boom-boom-**boom** . . . boom-**BOOM**!* went the drums.

"Faster!" Martin urged.

She leapt over branches. Slid down the track. Be wary of falling!

Boom!

She welcomed the aid of gravity. Perspiration half blinded her.

"Go!" Martin grated.

She navigated a final twist. The beach spread before her. Kicking sand, she raced for the whaleboat. Threw herself in amidst a flutter of skirts. Scrambled aft to avoid gear being pitched in behind her.

Martin and the men pushed the craft off the sand, then hurtled in themselves to work the oars. They were beyond spear throw when the wild band emerged from the trees and came roaring to water's edge.

Osa was no longer smiling. All right, they had survived this first incident. She knew that Martin would someday return to Malekula—and she with him. And she would be a different Osa by that time. A woman skilled not only with pistol but other firearms. She would have short hair. She would be wearing sturdy but cool trousers—no skirts flapping! And boots, not delicate slippers. Martin would never know that she had once feared snakes. She would be fluent in pidgin, and her smile—dear Lord—this new Osa would wear the dearest, most dependable, absolutely irresistible smile. . . .

Great sobs shook her, and she turned away so that none could see. But no one was paying attention, not even Martin. And the young woman resolved that any tears shed by Osa Leighty Johnson would always be private from this day on.

When Martin Johnson returned to Malekula almost two years later with a dozen armed men and a suitcase full of developed movie film, he brought a hard-eyed and trouser-clad Osa who was a crack shot with any firearm—a woman

far better equipped than before to face Chief Nagapate and his cohorts.

Arriving at sunset as planned for that second trip, Martin suspended from branches at the tree line above the beach a white sheet to use as a viewing screen. Then he projected film taken on the prior visit. Through pure luck, the footage included a tribesman who had died since the earlier visit. When Nagapate and the people of Malekula saw that man's features flashing before them, all believed the pale strangers to have what they considered Strong Magic. News of this marvel was indeed pounded by drum around the island; and safety among the Big Numbers was assured for the Johnsons and for any party they might in future bring to Malekula.

Filming adventure in the twenty years still to come, Martin and Osa Johnson became well known not only for the high quality of their work but also for the company they kept, including such personalities as Teddy Roosevelt, George Eastman and Carl Akeley. Safari lunches were taken with the Duke and Duchess of York, who went on to become King and Queen of England.

The Johnsons contributed much in their approach by camera to little-known places on earth.

"Probably no one ever wanted a real home more than I did," Osa wrote years later in *I Married Adventure* (still in print), one of her several books of memoir. "And no one *needed* one more than Martin." The Osa she became following the escape from Malekula was later known around the world as the tiny woman (not even five feet tall) who could make her home anyplace she and Martin happened to be. Her hospitality was celebrated. Her cool head and marksmanship not only sustained the camp but several times saved Martin's life—and that of others where she and they faced dangerous situations in the bush.

But even strong-willed, competent Osa could not avert the plane accident which seriously injured her and took Martin's life in 1937.

Osa *did* get her own home in the U.S. and live on until 1953, herself appearing on TV and even hosting a show to relate her adventures with Martin. In Chanute, Kansas, is located the Safari Museum as a tribute to the Johnsons and to house memorabilia from their travels.

Note: Martin Johnson was first cousin to the author's grandmother, Hester Jane Johnson Larkin of Beattie, Kansas.

Prior Publication

"Queen of Roar"
Contest Winner
Prior Publication by *Soundings Review (2012)*

"Beware the Fisher Cat"
Prior Publication by *Snowy Egret (2012)*

"While I Was Dead"
When Last on the Mountain
This story is in an anthology *The View from Writers over 50*
Edited by Vicky Lettmann and Carol Roan
Holy Cow! Press, (2010)

Acknowledgments

Nothing worthwhile springs into being without aid, at least not in my experience. And certainly this work garnered much support, tangible and abstract and sometimes from unexpected places . . . including unfailing help by Doug Bratten and now a second cover design by talented stepdaughter Irene Bratten Farrar and her also-artist husband Steve (23 Tons). The sculpture for the front cover of this Volume 2 is provided by also-talented stepdaughter Carolyn Bratten Boutwell. Many thanks are also accorded to the remarkable and long-time-friend Roberta Kirshner for sharing with me the often-colorful backgrounds of her exotic charges at the Barry R. Kirshner Wildlife Sanctuary and Educational Center (Chico, CA). And further, many thanks go to granddaughter Sultana Saritaş for the tiger photograph (also from Kirshner's) seen here on the back cover. Also on the back cover—and I am grateful!—is the author's picture taken and well photoshopped by Doug Bratten. Thus we have here "a family affair."

First among long-standing supporters in puissant ways (the actual writing) are members of SixMeet (Chico, CA) . . . Gary Briley, Clidean Dunn, Willa Perrine, Mike Sajben, and Jim Smith. Also due thanks are members of the TAT group (Wilton NH Library): Doug Bratten, Robert Ingraham, Richard Rasmussen, and Joan Tuttle.

Also, some recent and very helpful "read and reviewers" include Nancy DeMarco and J. E. Nissley with their critical eyes and Irene Hamilton with her unfailing encouragement—and certainly Paul Negri with his wise and practiced counsel. And of course—always!—Fran LesMoine.

Jenny Kay read my work for decades, dependably solid in her suggestions, unfailing with skilled aid. Mary Awa is the friend who encourages and aids with promotion—always interested, enthusiastic. And of course I can depend on Chicki Mallan, the long time friend and travel writer pro who speaks right up when asked and is usually right.

Certainly not to be forgotten are members of Claire Braz-Valentine's circle of writers who also have a hand in the finished product—notably Claire herself, Cindy McCusker, Chris Wood, George McClendon, Gloria Shogrun, Jenifer Bliss, and the late Bob Clark.

Some early rewrite in work is a result of suggestions from the Wednesday Writing Workshop (CA State University, Chico) connected through O.L.L.I. and including Velda Stubbings and Wanda Mathew-Woods along with 6Meet members who endured early versions of what is presented here.

Whatever errors occur are mine alone, stubbornly retained despite the cues and clues of the earnest helpers.

My immediate family, too, has provided support through unfailing encouragement: daughter Karol Saritaş who in a moment can call attention to any illogic, son-in-law Mah'mut Saritaş who—because I often merely file what I finish—cheerfully takes on faith that what I spend my time at is worthwhile. And son Kent Brisby with his wife Gingerlily who are always encouraging, ready to help. And of course the two granddaughters Sultana Saritaş (tiger photographer!) and Kalí Lowe-Brisby who are pleased to have Grandma Phyl busy without being on their cases and who both plan someday to read something ("short, please") that she's written.

And very special thanks go to so-knowledgeable Pam Marin-Kingsley and to long-suffering husband Doug Bratten— and to son Kent Brisby as well as granddaughter Sultana Saritas as we together venture into the unplumbed depths of Kalana Press.

Phyl Manning

About the Author
Phyl Manning

In her own words:

Yes, I'm a writer—and largely because of one humongous bag of potato chips! It must have been 1936 when the Omaha World Herald announced a Children's Poetry Contest. At five years old, I qualified. The newspaper even prescribed the title: "If I Could Fly." Whee-ee!

So yes, I rhymed up a poem of three verses: "If I could fly, I'd go up high/And catch hold of a cloud as it went by" and so forth. And my undistinguished literature won first place! So Kitty Clover Potato Chips (based in Omaha) rewarded me with a crisp new dollar bill AND the aforementioned bag of potato chips—a delicacy not experienced previously in those years of economic depression. Suddenly and permanently, I knew how to answer grownups who were always asking what I wanted to be when I grew up: a writer!